PRAISE FOR ERIK HATCH AND
PLAY FOR THE PERSON NEXT TO YOU

"Erik has been a huge chapter in my book of life! I have witnessed Erik's generosity, leadership, and heart for those around him firsthand. His ability to always see the best in others and his desire to create a community for everyone to thrive in has been an inspiration in my life. Erik goes out of his way to make a positive impact in the lives, businesses, and community surrounding him!"

—Rachel Johnson, COO, Hatch Coaching

"Erik Hatch is a difference maker. Erik is an energetic agent for change, growth, and positive impact in our world. His unique humor, honesty, and vulnerability make him an in-demand speaker and writer. Erik has a way of intimately connecting with people of all backgrounds through his seminars, writing, and one-on-one coaching. His unique life's journey has helped to shape him into a highly successful business owner and entrepreneur who is making a positive difference in our world. Let Erik share with you how to serve others by living passionately through your gifts and talents to positively impact the world."

—Rollie Johnson, Lay Pastor, First Lutheran Church (Fargo)

"Erik Hatch was just starting out in the real estate world and trying to shake hands and kiss babies when I met him. Despite his teddy bear appearance, Erik is a lion among lions. He has a vision of how leaders should lead, and it's transforming the business world. His generosity and transparency are refreshing. I would not follow many people, and I would happily follow Erik Hatch."

—Nick Shivers, CEO of West One Property Group & Cofounder of Sell a Home, Save a Child

"A true and inspirational leader, Erik stands apart from others with his unique way of generating joy and cultivating generosity. In both one-to-one conversations and in front of hundreds of people, Erik's authentic style of sharing his lived-experience insights encourages others to look outward and to engage in meaningful ways with their communities. His passion for servant leadership has led him to a life richly blessed in family, friendship, and career success, and he is compelled to share with you how it is possible to fully experience the life that we were born to live when we play for the person next to us."

—Kristi Huber, President & CEO, United Way of Cass-Clay (Fargo)

PLAY FOR THE PERSON NEXT TO YOU

ERIK HATCH

PLAY FOR THE PERSON NEXT TO YOU

A GUIDE TO SERVANT LEADERSHIP

Published by Advantage, Charleston, South Carolina.
Member of Advantage Media Group.

ADVANTAGE is a registered trademark, and the Advantage colophon is a trademark of Advantage Media Group, Inc.

Printed in the United States of America.

10 9 8 7 6 5 4 3 2 1

ISBN: 978-1-64225-100-5
LCCN: 2019911217

Book design by Megan Elger

This publication is designed to provide accurate and authoritative information in regard to the subject matter covered. It is sold with the understanding that the publisher is not engaged in rendering legal, accounting, or other professional services. If legal advice or other expert assistance is required, the services of a competent professional person should be sought.

Advantage Media Group is proud to be a part of the Tree Neutral® program. Tree Neutral offsets the number of trees consumed in the production and printing of this book by taking proactive steps such as planting trees in direct proportion to the number of trees used to print books. To learn more about Tree Neutral, please visit **www.treeneutral.com**.

Advantage Media Group is a publisher of business, self-improvement, and professional development books and online learning. We help entrepreneurs, business leaders, and professionals share their Stories, Passion, and Knowledge to help others Learn & Grow. Do you have a manuscript or book idea that you would like us to consider for publishing? Please visit **advantagefamily.com** or call **1.866.775.1696**.

For Emily, Finley, and Simon. You three are the most important people in my world, and you have forever changed my life.

CONTENTS

ACKNOWLEDGMENTS

People that declare themselves "self-made" are full of it. Whether through abundance or scarcity, our environments and surroundings cultivate the fruit that we bear. I am proudly a product of the people in my world that have refined and defined me.

Growing up, I didn't have a father that was active in my life— but I instead had two moms. I had my mom, Betty. She was a warrior of love that left this earth far too soon. And then I had my second mom—my aunt Anne. She lived a quick bike ride away but was as active in my life as any parent. Anne served her kids, her community, and hundreds of youth throughout the Fargo area for decades, and I was lucky enough to be one of those lives that she impacted. I got double the love from two amazing women for many years—and for that I am eternally grateful.

I also am lucky to have a plethora of siblings. My sister, Tanya, and I have found strength in each other through some tough days— and I'm really proud of the good she does in this world. And I have four cousins/siblings in Anne's kids. Shelley, Mark, Connie, and Deb are all massively successful in the ways in which they serve their families, their churches, and the world. While I may be the youngest of this bunch, I am confident I'm a product of their successes and failures.

First Lutheran Church in Fargo has played such an enormous role in shaping me. I was a dedicated church kid growing up and fell in love with serving through Rollie Johnson's leadership. He pushed me outside my box, showed up as the first real father figure in my life, and helped my faith come alive. I would follow him anywhere, and much of who I am is because of FLC and Rollie. Having the privilege to serve that congregation and the youth of Fargo and Moorhead for eight-plus years is one of the brightest spots in my life. I got paid to love God and serve people…What could be better? And now watching my kids grow up at that place gives me overwhelming joy!

God knew what I needed before I did—and surrounded me with amazing in-laws. Emily's family has become such a vital part of who I am. Sure, the free babysitting helps, too, yet it is an overwhelming gift to have Janie, Tom, Sandie, Maggie, Eric, Miles, and lots of others to experience life with. These are great people whose family I am obscenely lucky to have married into!

There have been dozens of people crazy enough to come and work for me. From my first hire (Mariah) to the eighty-first hire (and everyone in between), you all have trusted me with your professional and oftentimes personal lives. You have put the future of you and your families in my hands, and I have never taken that lightly. You are all my family, and I am committed to giving you everything I have each and every moment. I pray God uses me to help you be your best selves!

Finally, Emily. We were friends first before we ever fell in love. You were the breadwinner for years (as a first-grade teacher). You provided for us when I didn't have as much to contribute. And you continue to do so today. Sure, I've finally started carrying my weight financially—yet you still provide so much where I am inadequate. We are an unstoppable team and pretty fabulous parents (if I do say so). You are my everything. You are my partner in life, in business, and in faith. I am forever grateful.

ABOUT THE AUTHOR

Erik Hatch (Fargo, North Dakota) is an entrepreneur, public speaker, social media junkie, do-gooder, and servant leader. He has built eighteen businesses (and counting) in the last six years. From real estate to coaching, marketing to the nonprofit sector, and more, Erik is passionate about building businesses and people.

Erik's real estate team (the Erik Hatch Team) has been one of the top fifty real estate teams in the US since 2016. While the average Realtor sells roughly ten homes a year, the agents on Erik's team are helping nearly seventy families each on an annual basis. Erik's desire to create a movement of generosity among those he has the privilege of leading has created a massive ripple effect throughout the Fargo area.

Erik has spoken in front of groups of well over five thousand people and has been hired all over North America to inspire, entertain, and challenge. He has the gift of being able to make you laugh until you cry…and cry until you laugh. Companies such as Microsoft and the United Way and some of the top Realtors in North America have trusted Erik as a speaker and coach.

Erik has helped to build two different nonprofits in the last decade that have raised nearly $2.5 million (Homeless and Hungry and Sell a Home, Save a Child). He's bad at golf, great at eating bacon, and wonderful at losing his hair.

Erik's fingerprints can be found everywhere. He's a daring businessman and marketer. He's a powerful speaker. And he's committed to playing for the person next to him.

Do you know the feeling when someone magnetic enters a room? It's palpable. Whatever you're doing at the time ceases to matter; the conversation you're in takes a back seat. When a larger-than-life personality enters a room, your eyes immediately lock on this person, and you spend the next few moments watching the crowd of people flock around them as they try to catch a bit of their magic.

I was sitting in the back of a hotel ballroom in a small town in Minnesota. The year was 1998. The man I'm referring to with the magnetic nature was Erik Hatch. For the past twenty-plus years, I have watched Erik enter rooms, and the same thing happens every time. He does not burst across the threshold announcing, "Here I am!" Nay, Erik walks into a room, and you feel him saying, "There you are."

This is the great differentiator about the man whose book you are about to read. In a world where people are increasingly lured toward social media feeds that allow for endless self-praise and in a society that is trending toward self-centeredness, Erik Hatch is a classic, a throwback if you will. You see, Erik has built his life around serving others. That may sound cliché and seem like an overused platitude…until you see it in real life. To see Erik and the life he lives is to see a rare thing in this world because his life isn't about him—it's about others.

Do you know how good that makes me feel to know that my buddy Erik has used his time on earth to make an impact on people's lives?

Hatch and I have known each other since our teenage years, serving together in a volunteer organization called Key Club, the high school branch of Kiwanis. Even back then it was as if he knew service was his cornerstone. For twenty years I have witnessed Erik serving his community, giving back, and contributing to the lives of others. As we have grown up, experienced failure, found success, and done everything in between, Erik still teaches me lessons about life with each conversation we have. Erik is a brilliant man, driven and successful; however, he is still kind and caring and as thoughtful a man as I have ever met. The words you will read in the hours ahead have no doubt been agonized over in his own mind during sleepless nights as he considered how to best serve others.

The time you will spend reading this book, listening to his heart, and learning from his experience will be well spent for sure. However, my ultimate wish for you is that you one day find a friend like I have found in Erik Hatch.

All my best,

Mark J. Lindquist

*Mark J. Lindquist has been on the hottest shows on television (*Lost *and* Hawaii Five-0*), performs for the largest crowds in America (in the NFL, MLB, NBA, and NCAA), and speaks to the biggest companies on earth (McDonald's, Starbucks, Walmart, and Microsoft).*

INTRODUCTION

The irony is thick. Here I am writing a book, and my purpose in life is to be a chapter in everyone else's book. Years ago, searching for life's meaning in a conversation with a mentor, we found ourselves talking about how some people are but a couple of sentences in our lives while others are an entire section. Soon after we stumbled upon the words, "Be a chapter in everyone else's book," and they sent goose bumps down my spine. Instead of having my own amazing autobiography, wouldn't it be better to be a chapter in other people's books?

It was a moment of clarity. My calling in the world is not about *me*. It's about *we*. It's about serving others and making a difference. My real estate career has led me to experience some of the highest accolades and lowest valleys. I pursued so many things that weren't life giving or sustaining, and I've had the chance to digest what is really important.

This book challenges the standard business value that making money is always the primary goal. Don't misunderstand me—profit is absolutely necessary. However, I don't believe that the sole purpose of business is profit. Focusing your foundation on profit rather than relationships and connectivity with your team can be a recipe for disaster. Saying that profit is the primary function of having a business

Saying that profit is the primary function of having a business is like saying that breathing air is the primary function of living.

is like saying that breathing air is the primary function of living. Sure, it's essential to stay alive. Yet there's a lot more to life than breathing—and there's a lot more to business than making money.

Leaders have the opportunity to create something deeper than a business that focuses primarily on profit. From my own early failure in real estate, I learned that focusing solely on money and transactions can be toxic to workplace culture. When relationships come first, everything changes.

Nice guys can indeed finish first. You don't have to steamroll your way through business—leaving people in your wake at every turn. The following chapters will provide a plethora of examples of how champions can be developed through servant leadership. The best leadership to inspire people doesn't come from a position of authority. Rather, it comes from a position of connectivity and vulnerability. A leader's ability to slow down—to show their own brokenness—and to sincerely invest in the lives of those they have the privilege of serving can and will create more abundance than most conceive possible. When done correctly, those that serve will have the keys to the kingdom afforded to them.

When team members are acknowledged as whole people, they feel supported and empowered—and business thrives. Monetary success is a by-product of great service to our families and our teams. This book is about building genuine relationships that transform your life, your business, and the lives of the people around you. Simply put—relational is foundational.

When a servant leader truly finds their stride, they have the ability to zoom in and zoom out seamlessly. Zooming in includes walking alongside those in your care and doing life with one another. True listening, connection, and vulnerability are at the core of these relationships when a leader is zoomed in. Then that leader can effortlessly zoom out to make sure to see the entire picture and ensure that the decision making is handled with what's best for the group as the leading driver. All decisions are made while zooming in and zooming out with team members. When you're only zoomed out, you may fail to see the complexities and details that each person is influenced by. And when you're only zoomed in, it's near impossible to understand how the connections and bigger picture are impacted.

EARLY YEARS

In this introduction, I want to share a bit of my background so you can get to know me beyond my name and my businesses. In the spirit of building genuine, personal bonds with our team members, I want to start by sharing where I came from and what made me who I am as a person. As I'll discuss later in the book, who you are at work should not differ from who you are in real life.

I first learned about service and the importance of relationships from my mother and our church. I was raised in a single-parent home by my mother, Betty. My sister (Tanya, four years older) and I never really knew a life that involved our father, Larry. Our parents divorced when I was two, and he moved from our dumpy trailer in Argusville, North Dakota, to California, where he worked as a roofer. He would pop in every couple of years with a phone call or two sprinkled in. His absence provided an opportunity for my mom to become a superhero to us. Her power? Love and service.

My mom was tenacious. She worked her tail off, two or three jobs at a time, with the intent to provide for us the way a two-parent household would. (Our father did not pay much, if any, child support for seven years.) We moved to Fargo when I was five, and we had a small apartment we called home. Regardless of how much we struggled, my mom always spoke well of our dad. I was fortunate that she didn't play the blame game. Her positive attitude allowed me to feel that, even if I had a massive amount of animosity toward my father's absence, I never wished him any ill will.

When I was nine, my dad got knocked off a building by a wrecking ball and broke his back. He was medically discharged from working for the rest of his life, and that accident changed our situation back in Fargo: we received nearly seven years of unpaid child support, money that allowed us to pay off debt and move into a little townhome. This was my first taste of home ownership. Mom was as proud as the day is long buying a $49,000 house to take care of us.

MOM'S CANCER

When I was sixteen, I went to Mexico to do mission work with our church. On that trip my faith came alive for the first time, and I felt aligned with who God made me to be. Faith was no longer just something you did on a Sunday morning; it became the understanding of who I was designed to be—a servant, somebody who loved unconditionally and poured that love into others.

This book is about creating a business where relationships are integral to its success, but it's also about living a more purposeful life, discovering who we are as people, and understanding how we want to engage with the world. I had my first inkling of that as a sixteen-year-old in a foreign land. I thought I had life figured out. But when I arrived back in Fargo, I learned that my foundation at home was crumbling.

My mother told me, on the ride home from the airport, that she had been diagnosed with stage IV cervical cancer. She was given a 10 percent chance to live. As she battled for two years, she had but one wish: to see me graduate from high school. She had more chemotherapy and radiation than a human should ever have—as well as multiple surgeries—because her cancer was so serious. My sister was in the navy in San Diego, California, so I took on massive responsibility to care for Mom. In the mornings I often would clean her up and get her on the couch before I left for school. When I got home, I would make her dinner and clean up around the house before going to work for the night.

Yet she was really still taking care of me. Maybe not with her ability to tend to the small things, but she was taking care of me by showing what grit and tenacity really looked like. Those were monumental years for me. I learned from her what having a great faith and a great spirit and a great outlook on life really meant. By the time I graduated, the cancer was gone. In fact she didn't lose life; she gained life. She was even more vibrant than before.

Coming back from that mission trip, I understood who I really desired to be. Experiencing my mom's illness, caring for her, and witnessing what she demonstrated in the process gave me such an incredible outlook on life. I began to see the glass not as half-full or half-empty. I was just grateful to have a glass in the first place.

* * *

During my junior year of college at North Dakota State University, my friend Jonas and I ran for student body president and vice president. We were in the midst of a difficult campaign, and the day the election results came in announcing us as victorious, I got a call from Mom: the cancer had come back. That was April 2001, and she lived just two more months. My mother died that June, and I was a twenty-one-year-old orphan.

I had no idea where to go or what to do. But amid the chaos that was burning down my life, there were firefighters arriving to help. I began to see more clearly how much relationships truly matter. I had people from my church. I had people from my school. I had family members. These people didn't wait for an invitation. Like firefighters, they showed up because they saw someone that needed help. During one of the most difficult and lonely times in my life, I was surrounded by so much love and support. That, to me, is true servant leadership.

It took me a number of months to use that support to get my life together. The first six months after my mother's death, I used my hardship as an excuse. I played it small. Whatever was expected of me, I would say, "*Because* my mom just died…" to justify not doing it. I was a victim of the word *because*. It became my excuse for most everything.

By November of my senior year, I had had enough. I got on the treadmill at NDSU's wellness center the day before Thanksgiving. Something clicked in me that said, "I gotta start changing my stars." And for the first time in my life, I ran a mile. I was sweating gravy and au jus. Everything jiggled. It was painful. I wasn't proud of how I looked doing it, but I was immensely proud of finally showing up and pushing through the hard stuff. And this started a trend in my life of seeking out the pain and leaning into it rather than running away and hiding from it.

NO MORE EXCUSES

From there, I transformed my life and my health. I started working out, eating right, looking better, and feeling better. The next year I ran the Twin Cities Marathon. Pushing through the tough stuff was a way to honor my mother. The new me wasn't going to be someone who said, "*Because...*" I wanted to be someone who said, "*Even though...*": *Even though* my mom died, *even though* I grew up with fewer opportunities than some people, *even though* my father wasn't around, *even though* I was overweight and unhealthy, *even though* all these things had shown up in my life...I was no longer going to let any of that define me. I started paying attention to how true character was measured: showing up when nobody was watching.

When I was training for the marathon and thinking about my future, I decided I wanted to be a motivational speaker after graduation. I was drawn to having a microphone in my hand, and I knew that God had gifted me with some charisma, some energy, some humor, and the ability to be a good storyteller. I had already had a taste of motivational speaking through a company in Fargo that my youth pastor, Rollie Johnson, ran. He did retreats for kids based on the values of courage, compassion, integrity, and kindness. Through my mom's cancer and my faith coming alive, Rollie had become the closest thing I had to a father. He brought me in to be his sidekick for those retreats when I was twenty-one.

Rollie and I started visiting schools together, and I became an instant celebrity. The students thought I was the bee's knees. They thought I was the coolest guy because I told jokes and sang songs and played guitar and made them laugh. Those retreats helped them grow together, laugh together, express gratitude, heal, and find forgiveness. And they helped me to feel like I had purpose.

After graduating from NDSU, I was on the hunt for a job and had an opportunity to do these same kinds of retreats in Minneapolis, Minnesota. It was alluring, yet sage advice detoured my path. Rollie said to me, "Hatch, I know you. I have a feeling you're gonna be drawn more toward building relationships than doing a hit-and-run type of ministry." Motivational speaking was a hit-and-run kind of thing—in and out in a day. It fed my ego and gave me celebrity but did not build long-standing, deep relationships. Rollie was right. He offered me the chance to work with him at First Lutheran Church in Fargo as his full-time partner in youth ministry.

JOINING THE MINISTRY AND BECOMING AN ENTREPRENEUR

In 2003 I transitioned from bartending, which had put me through college, to working for the church. I took a 50 percent pay cut—a real reality check. I had worked in the bar and restaurant industry throughout high school and college, and now I was working for a nonprofit and becoming a nonprofit myself because I had no money.

Yet it was unbelievably fulfilling work. I was drawn toward relationships and connecting, and I found joy in being a lot to a little. I got to be the person my mom was for me: the person who breathed possibilities into kids and showed them courage and resilience. The church invited me in to love people in some of their hardest times— to align with them without waiting for permission but rather to run toward them. I was no longer interested in trying to be everything to everyone (although my ego sometimes told me I wanted that). It was in the deep-rooted relationships that I found the most value. Some of my closest friends today are the kids I worked with while an employee of the church.

My eight years in the ministry also taught me entrepreneurship. I had the chance to create new things within the four-thousand-plus person organization that was First Lutheran Church. We did seven different "Mystery Mission Trips"

> *It was in the deep-rooted relationships that I found the most value.*

where kids signed up without knowing where they were going or what they were going to do. (We told their parents of course.) We'd put forty or fifty kids on a bus, and they'd wake up the next morning in somewhere like Laredo, Texas. We'd work for a week, and the kids would come home inspired and challenged to be better for the world. Perhaps most significant was another endeavor the kids and I created together: the Homeless and Hungry Movement, which ultimately ran for ten years and raised over one million dollars to fight homelessness in Fargo. (The Homeless and Hungry Movement will be discussed more in chapter 3.) We also created an ecumenical worship service that was run out of a pizzeria and comedy club, drawing together unchurched people as well as bringing many denominations together in one space. It was a different way to do church. We laughed hysterically, we occasionally sang Taylor Swift songs, and we gave a voice to the broken to share their stories.

The church was an entrepreneurial playground for me, and there was a blissful ignorance that came from working with young people. I crave that terribly still. I could say to these kids, "You can dream big. You can go and change the world. We'll find a way to get there." They were naive enough to believe me—not because they had a lack of intelligence but because they hadn't yet been burned by the world. They didn't have a whole bunch of *because* excuses. Adults think we know what we're doing, but adopting the mindset of innocence and blissful ignorance clears the path for so much more opportunity.

MEETING MY WIFE AND GETTING INTO REAL ESTATE

Just a few months after starting at the church, a tall blond woman caught my eye. Emily was in college and volunteering at our church. We soon developed crushes on each other, but I had set a rule for myself that I was never going to ask out somebody from church for fear of ruining their relationship with God. I didn't want to be creepy Erik hitting on someone and keeping them from Jesus. My wife is quite shy, yet after about six months, she had the courage to say to me, "Erik, why don't you like me?" I told her that I did and then soon asked for a first kiss to "get it out of the way." She laughed in my face—and I knew it was true love.

We got married at the church in 2006, and two weeks later Emily was hired to be a first-grade teacher. After a few years of marriage, we started talking about wanting to start a family. Unfortunately we weren't able to get pregnant right away. We were put on a sex schedule, which sounded awesome. It was not, and it didn't work. We then went through a few rounds of intrauterine insemination (IUI). That didn't work either. Our health insurance covered this expense—but only up to a point. When we ran out of insurance coverage and still weren't pregnant, we had a decision to make. I was a part-time Realtor (I got my real estate license in 2006 to earn some extra cash) and a full-time church worker, and we didn't have enough money to fund the necessary in vitro fertilization (IVF) treatments.

In early 2011 we made the decision for me to move full time into real estate so we could fund our prayer of being parents.

I went into the real estate business simply to make money. Oddly, it was never a passion. I knew nothing about houses, and to this day I still don't know much about them. (Up until a few years ago, I didn't know that Sheetrock and drywall were the same thing.) I had no understanding of real estate in terms of brick and mortar, but my previous profession working for the church had helped me understand people. While I wasn't passionate about real estate, I was and still am passionate about people. And that's really what real estate is about. It has nothing to do with houses and everything to do with the people who are living in a home. I had accumulated years of experience without ever knowing it.

LEARNING FROM FAILURE

This book is about a kind of leadership that goes beyond transactions to forming genuine relationships and allowing team members to be their full selves. This approach to business is often talked about but rarely executed. When you lead this way, you create a culture where motivated people *want* to work. I learned these lessons from my first experience building a team, which I did entirely the wrong way.

In 2011, in hopes of being a dad, I went into real estate full time and experienced quick success. The average Realtor nationwide sells between six and ten homes a year; in my first year, I sold fifty-two houses and was one of the top Realtors in Fargo. The next year I took the leap and started a team because that's what many of us are told to do: if you're good at selling homes, go build a team and lead people. This makes about as much sense as saying, "Hey, you're good at algebra, so you should go start a bowling league." Sales and leadership are two entirely different skill sets. I ended up starting a team with no business acumen and no real idea of how to lead people in a setting like this. If you raised your hand, I hired you. I had no clue what I was doing.

As a team, we grew quickly. By the end of 2012, we were thirteen people "strong." In 2012, of the 192 homes that my team sold, I sold 113. That many homes sold by a team had people taking notice, but it was Erik and the Rockettes. I didn't care about other people's success nearly as much as I should have. I simply wanted the accolades and their support. Even saying this now feels nasty, and the result wasn't surprising: people quit. Yet my ego wouldn't let me see what I was doing wrong. I had gotten away from why I had gone into real estate full time—to earn enough to have a family. I had developed the desire to have a big life and a big business and be important. I had become self-centered.

My team's early success had nothing to do with quality. In fact the quality of service we gave our clients was disgraceful—especially based on how we conduct our business today—as was the quality of service I gave my team members. I am ashamed that I had them working for me and I wasn't working for them. I was concerned only about my success; their success didn't cross my mind. I just thought my table scraps would be enough for them.

Unfortunately there are a lot of businesses, real estate and otherwise, built that way. There's great success for the person at the top, but how can you have a fulfilling life when your team members are left trying to figure out how *they're* going to make a living? I had no idea how much of a dumpster fire I had created when, in April 2013, I got called in to meet with the team leaders. They told me it wasn't working anymore. They released me from the company. That's the political way to say it, really. It felt like I was fired, kicked out, rejected, and despised. My ego (I was their top salesperson—and frankly I thought I was bulletproof) was crushed, and my soul was broken. And it was all my fault.

I was fired for the first and only time in my life. Up until then I had always been the suck-up, sit-in-front, goody-two-shoes church guy. Yet I had become toxic and destructive without even realizing it. After getting let go, I met with my team and invited them to come with me to a new brokerage. Of the thirteen people who worked for me, only one agent and one admin came along. The rest said something along the lines of "Erik, you are more of a liability than an asset at this point." That was an even more shocking wake-up call for me than getting fired. The people I thought were aligned with me—the people I thought were in my corner—actually were not. Why? Because I wasn't in their corner.

TREATING PEOPLE DIFFERENTLY: HATCH REALTY IS BORN

My character had rightfully been called into question. I was far from the guy who had gone to work for the church to make a difference. I had become self-centered and focused on money/transactions as the ultimate measure of success. Getting fired gave me the gift of starting over. I joined a new brokerage. For nine months I ate nothing but humble pie. I decided to take the lessons I had learned, clean my wounds, go through the fire, and build a real team.

In January 2014 we opened Hatch Realty. I turned down the noise from outsiders and started paying attention to my insiders. Every day my job was to take care of my team and our clients. In the words of Zig Ziglar, I knew that I could have everything I wanted if I helped other people get what they wanted. I was dedicated to showing up differently as a leader and building a company that was different from every other real estate company out there. Five years later, in 2019, we find ourselves as one of the top fifty teams in the country for the fourth straight year. When asked how many people work for me, I say none. Yet I have thirty-five people at Hatch Realty whom I work for every day.

Hatch Realty is a place where people become who they never thought possible. We're a training ground for leadership and love and character because we pay attention to the soul of the person much more than transactions. I don't call the people I work with employees; they're my team members, and they're my family. These principles also guide Hatch Coaching, my business coaching company that is striving to redefine how people treat people. When you build and lead a business that acknowledges people for who they truly are, the result is a deeper sense of purpose for everyone involved.

I don't call the people I work with employees; they're my team members, and they're my family.

Building real relationships with team members creates a thriving workplace and a more purposeful life. The things we know about our team members have little to do with just the dollars they want to make or the number of homes they want to sell. We know the kind of family they want to have, the loss they have experienced, and what kind of person they want to be. We know their deepest, darkest motivators. This depth of relationship with your team requires you to lead not in a one-size-fits-all way, but in a customized, personal way.

* * *

I grew up watching *Boy Meets World* on TV. This charming and cheesy sitcom tells the story of Cory and his best friends, Shawn and Topanga. Upon graduating from high school, these three seek out their mentor/neighbor/principal/teacher (all the same guy), Mr. Feeny, for some final wisdom.

Topanga: "We wanted to know if you have anything else you wanted to teach us."

Mr. Feeny: "Believe in yourselves. Dream. Try. Do good."

Topanga: "Don't you mean do well?"

Mr. Feeny: "No, I mean do good."

And there it is. *Do good.* Serve. Everything else is secondary.

CHAPTER 1

THE PURPOSE OF A SERVANT LEADER

On January 12, 2010, my worldview changed forever. Everything in me shook as an observer, as somebody who was watching from the outside. That day, the people of Haiti experienced the most destructive natural disaster in the history of their country. Over 230,000 people died as a result of that earthquake. And prior to that day, Haiti was already the most poverty-stricken country in the Western hemisphere.

I saw coverage of the earthquake pass across my news feed, and while most of the time I would sit idly by, this time I didn't. We are so inundated with noise and destruction and violence when we turn on the news that we're almost numb to it. But not this time for me. I realized I felt called to do something, and so I rallied together a group of fifteen young adults from my congregation. We decided to go to Haiti that August.

Now, I sweat a lot already. But going to Haiti in August was maybe the sweatiest decision I've ever made. Everything was hot. The country was so heavy with death and poverty and heat that my whole being felt weighed down. It was hard to breathe—emotionally and physically.

We served at the Son of God Orphanage in Carrefour, Haiti. When we arrived, we made our way through narrowing hallways (the walls had moved in the earthquake) and entered a large room where we were immediately grabbed by children. They clung to us for any source of love and possible rescue. My heart broke knowing that we couldn't rescue those kids. Yet I knew that, for a few days, we could love them and spend quality time together.

I ended up meeting a young boy named Jhon. He didn't speak English, and I didn't speak a lick of Creole. Yet we shared a language of love, affection, and playfulness together. I would point at something on his shirt and then boop him on the nose, and he would giggle pretty uncontrollably. I would tap him on the shoulder, he would look one way, and I would laugh because of course I was on the other side. During our second day at the orphanage, Jhon wrestled away a comb from another child and started combing my hair to show affection. If you've never met me, I have quite the receding hairline, so his efforts were out of love and not necessity. While laughing, I said to him, "Jhon, Jhon, Jhon," and pointed to my face, and he started combing my beard. I was laughing; he was laughing. Then I pointed to my arm. More combing, more laughter. It was peculiar and hilarious. Testing my limits, I said to him, "Jhon, Jhon, Jhon," and pointed to my chest hair. Without hesitation, he started combing my chest hair! We both laughed until our eyes welled with tears. Our bond was wonderfully special and fun.

But remember, it's August in Haiti. It was crazy hot. And in the room there were 125 orphans along with us Americans and no air circulation. Jhon saw how much I was sweating, so he went and found a paper plate and started trying to fan me. It was such a weird, surreal moment to have an eight-year-old orphan choose to try to take care of me. While his fan didn't really cool me off, I sure appreciated the gesture.

But it was the next moment I'll never forget. Jhon took my arm, brought it up to his face, and then slowly blew his breath onto my skin. It cooled me down immediately and gave me goose bumps all over my body. This boy was going through tougher times than you or I will probably ever experience in our lives, yet he showed up as a servant for me. I thought it was my job as an American who came from abundance and privilege to serve Jhon and the other orphans, but this young man understood servant leadership to the core. He took the time to invest in me.

It took an eight-year-old Haitian orphan to show me what leadership looked like. It wasn't about title or power. It was about love and service.

I believe that when you take the time to go out of your comfort zone to serve someone else, you're going to find that it's you who gets served in the process.

LEAVING THE CHURCH

When I got back from Haiti, my wife and I were in the midst of trying to conceive. We recognized that my career at the church was coming to an end, but my desire to serve was completely heightened by my time in Haiti. I knew that I wanted to bring the spirit of service into whatever I did next.

In 2011 I left my job as a youth director and went full time into real estate. I had a family to start, and financial gain was imperative. First Lutheran Church in Fargo had meant everything to me. I was baptized and raised there, I buried my mom there, and I married Emily there. It was the place that gave me family and inclusion during the toughest times of my life. And it was the place I had worked at for eight years after college.

Working at the church provided the community and family I so desperately craved. The church was flowing with opportunity to grow, but the most difficult part was working within the infrastructure of a large organization that told a guy like me to slow down. I felt called to run fast, run often, and sniff around in areas that hadn't been sniffed before. That is really difficult for any large organization to embrace. The church served me in so many amazing ways, and my passions and my *purpose* both grew. But there came a time when I felt called to be my own boss—to run fast and sniff out new opportunities. I wasn't running from something; I was running toward something.

THE OXYGEN MASK LESSON

What does it mean to be a servant leader? It means taking a continuous look at what's best for the group and the individuals (in that order) and acting upon that. This idea didn't happen on accident; I came to understand it as a way to take care of my team and have success in business. Servant leaders are able to show genuine support for individuals while making decisions that benefit the whole. In addition to acting in the best interest of the entire team, servant leaders operate from a deep sense of purpose. They do not lead solely to build a business, transact with customers, and make money. Their purpose is deeper than that.

Leaders have a high level of responsibility to those in their care. To do servant leadership right, others come before self. The decisions I make *do* impact me, of course, because my life is directly tied to the business that I have the privilege of leading, but rarely does "what's best for me" enter my mind. With that said, servant leaders *do not* ignore their own needs. They take excellent care of themselves so they're able to serve others.

The ability to serve others to the highest level requires a servant leader to first take care of his or her own well-being. Picture a pyramid cut in cross sections: the base is God, self, and family; the next section up is team; above that is clients; and the top of the pyramid is community. Many times, I've gotten my pyramid out of whack and put my team or clients or community first. I've forgotten to take care of myself and my family. But those things are the foundation of your pyramid, and we can't ignore them. I used to have guilt about taking care of myself—for working out, getting a massage, or reading a book. But if my pyramid is in

order, then I'm taking care of myself, my God, and my family first. Although we're serving others, it cannot be at the cost of our own health. (This pyramid and priorities in general are covered in more detail in chapter 5.)

I learned this when I was Jhon's age, eight years old, and got on a plane for the first time to visit my father in California. Prior to takeoff, I paid diligent attention to the flight attendant giving instructions. She talked about how, in case of an emergency, an oxygen mask would drop down, and she instructed us to put on our masks first before helping others. At first I questioned what she was saying because my mom had always talked about taking care of others. Later I began to understand how sensible it was. If you're ever going to help someone else, you have to put on your own oxygen mask first.

> *If you're ever going to help someone else, you have to put on your own oxygen mask first.*

SERVANT LEADERSHIP IN ACTION

Servant leadership is often talked about yet rarely demonstrated. I try to improve on it daily, but I still feel like a novice in this journey because I see the ultimate example in Jesus Christ and how he lived his life. Most days I'm left staring at two sides of a pendulum: one side is grace; the other is the hard edge of business. If I'm trying to figure out how to be the best servant leader I can possibly be, I have to understand that it can mean making tough decisions that don't necessarily sit well with everyone. I'm learning that both grace and authority should exist in the workplace. It's not a problem; it's a polarity. Grace doesn't cease to exist because authority is necessary (and vice versa). Rather, these two coexist in harmony—even though they're sometimes seen as polar opposites of each other.

A servant leader struggles knowing that someone or a small group won't benefit. Intrinsically this is tough. But it's part of the responsibility we have to those in our care. Servant leaders have the ability to zoom in, analyze up close what's best for the person, and then zoom out to see what the consequences are for the whole team. We sometimes wrongly think that, as a servant, it's always our duty to help every individual person, to lie down for them whenever they ask. But we can't take "being a servant" so literally. To serve does not mean letting someone walk all over you. I've been close to that line; I've let the pendulum swing too far toward grace, and people have taken advantage of situations.

I can't just do what's right for one person when my responsibility is to see the entire puzzle. My job is to piece together everything. Consider why parents discipline their kids. They love them enough to discipline them because addressing problematic behavior is important to the entire family. Similarly, servant leaders bring grace and love. They also maintain that edge in order to act for the benefit of the entire team.

*   *   *

When we had the privilege of opening Hatch Realty in 2014, it came after a number of mistakes: getting kicked out of a previous brokerage, making huge financial blunders, and stumbling my way through leadership. My early approach in real estate was all about me. It was Erik and the Rockettes. I failed miserably and lost nearly my entire team in the process. Since crashing and burning, I now find myself surrounded by more abundance than I ever thought possible. I now work for my team, and they are immensely successful.

I was fortunate to get a second chance. I knew that we had to be a different kind of company and that I had to be a different kind of leader. We couldn't just be about real estate, so we sprinkled in things that would provide our team members with deeper levels of satisfaction—things that would speak to people's love languages and allow folks to feel that they could live out their passions at their work home. I didn't see that kind of work environment anywhere else.

We have four different kinds of team members at Hatch Realty: agents/salespeople, inside sales agents (ISAs), showing/listing partners, and administrators. As their servant leader, I want all of them to not only be taken care of but to thrive beyond what they thought was possible. That means something different for each position. Salespeople are independent contractors with a high financial glass ceiling; ISAs and partners are part salary, part commission, so their glass ceiling is a bit more limited; and our admin staff operates on salary or hourly pay plus other benefits. We measure success across all four groups, valuing things like the purpose we work for, retention rates, and the enrichment of the lives of our team members. For me, that's where I can sit back and say that we have done well for those in our care. The number of transactions we close does matter. The profit we make does matter. Yet the lives our team members get to live and the impact they make on this world are the ultimate measures of success.

Every single salesperson who works for Hatch Realty had no formal real estate experience prior to joining us. Today nearly every one of them is earning two, three, four, or five times as much as they were previously. Those resources have allowed them to start families and purchase homes. They have also built genuine relationships that have expanded their lives. This was not just my doing of course. These folks came into our world with the ability to be fantastic. My job was to show them how capable they are.

My job is to help those in our world to fly—and so I am in the business of helping them to build runways. A great leader doesn't have to outfly everyone. Rather, a great leader should help build a runway to help others soar. We train exceedingly well. We connect deeper than most anywhere else. We listen intently to what our team wants. And together we help them fly. If someone is building a runway with you and for you, don't you think you'll fly high—and fly far—and then return to that same airport?

* * *

I was at an event once featuring John Maxwell, and someone from the crowd asked him, "John, how do you motivate your team members?"

He replied, "I don't."

The questioner was confused. "What do you mean you don't motivate your team members?"

Maxwell said, "I don't motivate my team members because I hire motivated people."

At Hatch Realty and Hatch Coaching, we make sure the people who come into our world already have a fire inside them. My job is to provide kindling, air, and fanning. It's not my job to light a fire in somebody; it's my job to help that fire burn more powerfully. Over the last seven years, when we look at the success of people who have come through our system, every Realtor who started with us is still in real estate. People have stayed and had massive lives they couldn't have afforded otherwise. Others have started their own gigs and become exceedingly successful, and I have a sense of pride knowing I was a contributor to their success.

Because administrators don't have the same financial glass ceiling as our agents and ISAs/partners, we make sure we're paying attention to other things in their lives. We give our admin team unlimited time off and the freedom to never have to punch a clock; we give them autonomy and ownership within their job. We also give them a culture that radiates energy and positivity. In our world people tend to hate Fridays and love Mondays.

RESULTS OF SERVANT LEADERSHIP

In our little city of Fargo, Hatch Realty has captured large amounts of market share and mindshare—and done so quickly. We are successful not only in terms of sales numbers but more so in the kind of growth, energy, and love we have. Some businesses have a lot of transactions, but their work is parched of purpose. It's not fulfilling because it's not putting enough focus on the valuable connections between team members.

> *Some businesses have a lot of transactions, but their work is parched of purpose.*

In contrast, there's a group mentality in our world. For example, when we have open positions, we do an invitation-only career night prior to ever interviewing a single candidate. We usually have two or three dozen people show up. From moment one, we set the stage, sharing with them the passion of our organization. We talk about what's most important in our world and how deeply we care about our families and team members. The clients don't come first; our families and God come first. After that, it's still not the client—it's our team members. We make sure that we're taking care of one another, which puts everyone in the best possible position to go out and take care of clients.

Our group mentality is articulated from the first moment people step into our company. A sign in our training room, where we hold career night, reads, "*We're in the business of helping people...we just happen to sell real estate.*" We make sure that same message radiates throughout the walls of our building each and every day. We ensure that we're giving people the permission and space to be their best selves. We believe that being our best selves happens when we serve those around us rather than waiting for people to serve us. It's that idea of bearing fruit: making sure that everyone else has enough to eat rather than just paying attention to what we're consuming.

Our team members all have the willingness to be servants for one another. This culture must be protected. If you allow one person in who isn't a servant, toxicity can result. There's a scene in the movie *Caddyshack* where all the caddies gather at the pool one afternoon. Everybody is enjoying themselves and having a great time until a Baby Ruth gets thrown in the water. It's only a candy bar, but merely the sight of something that looks like a turd makes everybody run. You can have thousands of gallons of crystal clear, chlorinated pool water, but add one thing that even remotely looks like a turd and you just have shitty water. Nobody wants to be around it.

If you have a group of servants and one taker, people will run from them. We can't let in anyone who is not a servant, who is different from the rest of us in this respect. We have to protect our workplace culture with that kind of intensity.

You can have thousands of gallons of crystal clear, chlorinated pool water, but add one thing that even remotely looks like a turd and you just have shitty water.

STANDARDS, GOALS, EXPECTATIONS

Like John Maxwell, we hire motivated people. And once on board, *their* goals drive everything.

Picture a sheet of paper with three words written on it: centered at the bottom of the page is "Standards," in the middle is "Goals," and at the top is "Expectations." Standards are those baseline things that everyone has to adhere to. It's the bare minimum; you have to be above that in order to play in our world. We've created exceedingly high standards—higher, in fact, than almost anyone in the industry. Our standards are so high because we have a culture where greatness is bred.

Goals are not the goals of the company. These are the goals of the individual agents, ISAs/partners, and administrators on our team. *Their* goals are what we hold them accountable to. My business coach, Steve Kout, once told me that you can hold someone accountable to *your* goals and they'll resent you, or you can hold them accountable to *their* goals and they'll thank you. We talk at length with our team members about what we're helping them to chase. Together, we define what they need to do to reach their goals. As a team we encourage and support one another to attain those goals. We hold them accountable to what is most important to them.

I believe that the embracing of high expectations, at the top of the page, is the reason our agents and ISAs have had so much success. Society often tells us, "Don't have high expectations because people will let you down" or "Lower your expectations so you'll never be disappointed." The message is to keep your expectations in check or marry your expectations to someone else's goals.

But my job is to remind my team of what they are actually capable of. When I worked with kids, I could tell them that they could go and change the world, and they were so innocent and not yet scarred that they believed me. And sure enough, many would go and do so. Now, as a business owner, my job is still the same. I'm called to inspire belief in those around me—that they can be so much more than they ever thought. We create an environment that reminds them of what's possible rather than what their scarred, tattered experiences have taught them. We expect them to be great, and we remind them of that daily. I'm confident that those I work for every day can go and change the world. I simply need them to be innocent and naive and ignorant enough to believe it. Then they can go and do just that!

EXPECTATIONS

GOALS

STANDARDS

RICHES VERSUS WEALTH

In my first year in real estate full time, I quintupled my income. It was striking how it made me feel: ashamed. My phrase for it was "wealth guilt." Yet, at the same time, I was enamored with it. Transitioning from a nonprofit church into an entrepreneurial venture like real estate, the amount of wealth it created was astounding to me. Because I was now able to afford things I never had before, I held the false assumption that my heart had to change with it. So I pursued riches. It still made me feel guilty, but for a while I measured success based on the amount of money in my checking account.

Eventually I learned that that mindset doesn't provide anything close to lasting fulfillment. Riches are indeed measured by what's in your checking account. Wealth is very different. Wealth is an abundance of resources—money, yes, but also two other critical pieces: time and culture. And these three only matter when they are rooted in purpose—clarity of why we do what we do. *Time* means you have the opportunities to live the life you want instead of being a slave to your career. You're not sacrificing family, relationships, or other things that matter to you for the pursuit of money. *Culture* means the community that you've created around you, surrounding yourself with people who are like-minded, quality folks with whom you can dream and be your best selves.

> *Wealth is an abundance of resources—money, yes, but also two other critical pieces: time and culture. And these three only matter when they are rooted in purpose—clarity of why we do what we do.*

I believe that if you have one or two of these, but not all three, then genuine life fulfillment is not possible. Money, time, and culture together create an environment for people to lead bigger lives with higher production and happiness. I've been down the road of pursuing money, which so many people have done and are still doing. In the beginning of my real estate career, it was all about the money, and I was miserable. I wasn't concerned about the time in my day or the culture I was creating. My impact wasn't real because it was only for me.

So many people are chasing that false idol of riches thinking it's going to bring them everything they want. We need to pursue wealth instead, which means we can't just chase after transactions; we have to chase after value and purpose. The wealthiest, most successful people in this world have an abundance of money and time, and they are ingrained in the right culture. Their lives are enriched with purpose. All these together lead to the highest amount of fulfillment and impact.

OUR CALL IS TO GIVE—AND GIVE GENEROUSLY

When I worked at the church, I had a great culture, limited time, and no money. I tried to figure out how I could give with those resources. Too often, I made the excuse that, because I had limited means, I should not be expected to give. I justified this by reasoning that rich people should be the ones cutting the checks for charity. I found excuses to not give, deciding that my little treasure was for me to hang on to.

Hatch Realty was built on the idea that we were going to be more than just real estate. We were going to serve with the hearts of those who run nonprofits. I was going to share my profits with my team, so we fundamentally give up 25 percent of our profits to our team members. We also made the decision that we wanted to take care of our community, so we fundamentally give up 25 percent of our profits to invest in charities that we believe in. That leaves my wife and me with fifty cents on the dollar of profit, pretax. We did that knowing it was the kind of company we would want to work for and would be proud of owning.

Ultimately I think we're all called to give—and give generously. These good works are set aside for us, whether it be giving to your church, if that's your thing, or your community, or nonprofits, or all of the above. We have this opportunity to show up and be consistent servants. That happens when we make a commitment to our financial resources instead of putting it off. I can't tell you how many times I've heard people say that they are going to give; they're just waiting for the right day to come. Magically the clock will strike midnight, and they'll become a giver. But the way to become a generous giver is to be a giver in the first place. You can't just show up one day and be a generous giver. It takes massive amounts of intention and time. As a servant leader, you should always be investing with the intent to multiply.

CHAPTER 2

MULTIPLY

Everything Is Contagious

One of the most difficult jobs on earth is working with middle schoolers at a required church event. When I was a youth director, I would have six kids who were excited to be there and sixty who absolutely did not want to be there. If they were playing in the gym, they loved that; if we were doing a Bible lesson, they really checked out. We had to find a way to get them interested. We knew that if we could get their attention, we could start injecting some real life and faith stuff into them, so my first goal was to befriend the kids—not to talk about faith but instead to talk about life.

As we started to build trust and rapport with one another, they began asking questions about their purpose in life. Some of my favorite scripture comes from Ephesians. Ephesians 2:8 (New International Version) is a well-known verse: "For it is by grace you have been saved, through faith—and this is not for yourselves, it is a gift of God." Most people stop after Ephesians 2:9, which continues, "… not by works, so that no one can boast." People think, "Thank goodness I'm saved by grace through faith. I didn't do anything to deserve it. It's a gift that's been given to me." But if you keep reading, Ephesians 2:10 hits you right between the eyes: "For we are God's handiwork, created in Christ Jesus to do good works, which God prepared in advance for us to do."

This verse says there are good works set aside for us to do, and that's what we're designed for—*that's* our life purpose. Many times as a youth director, kids came to me confused about what life is really supposed to be about. I often referred to this verse, and it always provided clarity. These kids didn't know if they were going to be a construction worker, a nurse, or an architect. I told them, "It doesn't matter what you do as a profession, but it does matter what you do as a servant. We're created to do good works that are already prepared for us."

* * *

Every year, my team and I attend a simulcast of the Global Leadership Summit, which is put on by Chicago's Willow Creek Church and is broadcasted all over the world to churches, prisons, and everywhere in between. The majority of us attend the two-day summit to get poured into by the speakers. There's a grand potpourri of speakers like Colin Powell, Simon Sinek, and Marcus Lemonis. This event has been a major cornerstone in my personal development. For me, there's a merging together of faith and life. They are no longer two separate things; it's all just one thing.

At the summit four years ago, I ran into one of my youth group kids. Dan is a worship pastor in Fargo. When I saw him, I knew that he and his wife had just welcomed their third child under the age of four. I gave him a big, grizzly bear hug and asked how he was doing. "I'm doing pretty well," he said with a smile. "God's first commandment is to be fruitful and multiply, so I am taking Him literally on that." We had a good laugh. Church humor…am I right?!

But from that moment, the word *multiply* became a theme I would hear over and over again throughout the summit. The word has special resonance for my family (I'll get to that below), but until Dan's comment I didn't realize how *multiply* was infusing its way into the everyday language I heard around me. Many people at the summit were talking about more abundance, more generosity, and more servanthood. On the second day, over lunch, I told my team that I kept hearing this theme of *multiply*. I told them that I felt my life was meant to be more than just what I was doing; I felt that it was meant to be multiplied for other people. I didn't know what I was supposed to do with it, I said, but I knew it was personal for me and that I was inspired by it and called to it.

The theme of multiply was certainly personal for my wife and me. We battled infertility for five years before welcoming our daughter, Finley, into the world in October 2014. When she was born—because it was such a special moment after trying for so long to have a baby—we hired my friend Lindsay, a videographer, to join us for the labor and birth. As Lindsay was editing the birthing video, she called me to ask about a theme song. My wife and I talked about it, and the song "Multiplied" by Needtobreathe had become our anthem. Even before we welcomed Finley, our life had already been multiplied when Emily and I came together. Our daughter's birth meant it was multiplying from there.

Quite often, when we add something to our lives, we create more of the core of what we are naturally designed for, so what we're doing is not adding but multiplying. After sharing with my team how I felt called to the theme of multiply, I walked back to the summit with one of my team members, Kyle. He was in his midtwenties at the time, young and hungry, blissfully ignorant as to what impossibilities are, and hopelessly optimistic about what could be. Kyle told me that he wanted to become a giver in his life and, when he was thirty, wanted to donate $100,000 to nonprofits.

"That moment," he said, "that donation, when I'm able to donate one hundred thousand dollars to charity, will change my life."

I told Kyle I thought it was a fantastic plan, and I offered an idea: what about easing into it so it becomes something sustainable—something that isn't a one-and-done but something that you will continue for the rest of your life? Together, we came up with a plan: At twenty-seven, he would donate $10,000. At twenty-eight, he would donate $30,000. At twenty-nine, he would donate $60,000. And at thirty, he would donate $100,000. That would be $200,000 donated over four years. This brief conversation revealed something amazing for me: having simply told my team what my heart was telling me about multiplying, Kyle's response made me feel like that multiplication was already happening.

Back at the summit, we were given some lead-in questions and encouraged to start journaling. If you know anything about event programming, you know the second day after lunch is the hardest slot to fill. People are lethargic and usually in a food coma if you do it right. For me, that usually means a chance to check Facebook or get caught up on emails that have been piling up throughout the day. But after hearing about Dan's third child, after talking over lunch about the idea of multiplying, and after having the conversation with

Kyle on the walk back, I was in it. I didn't want to lose the feeling and momentum.

One of the lead-in questions included the word *multiply*. It was something along the lines of, "What from your life do you want to be multiplied into this world?" At that moment, the house band, which had been playing melodic music while we were journaling, began to play Needtobreathe's "Multiplied." The theme came full circle, and I sat there weeping tears I hadn't cried in a decade. I was overrun with emotion because I felt clarity around what my purpose was supposed to be: my life is meant to be multiplied. I understood that the love that I show and the care that I give *can* be multiplied for other people. I saw that seed already planted in Kyle. When I was bold enough to talk about living a big, over-the-top, audacious life, Kyle came right alongside and said, "I want that too."

US, CLIENTS, LOCAL, GLOBAL: MULTIPLY THE IMPACT

I had this overarching clarity about my life's mission, but I had no idea how to start living that. I did know that I wanted to involve my team members. The week after the summit, I sent a group text to our staff: "If you feel called to be a part of something bigger, join us at 11:00 a.m. on Thursday." At that point, my team was around thirty people; two-thirds of them showed up. I had no idea what I was going to do, but I knew that I felt inspired to multiply and that I had to start putting it out there. Instead of living in the shadows and quietly having my dreams, I knew I needed to be bold and audacious with what I felt called toward.

As everyone gathered that Thursday morning, I shared with them my experience at the summit, how on fire I was, and how I had wept tears of life's clarity. And then I simply invited them to come alongside and multiply with me. After witnessing Kyle's response, I knew that the idea of multiplying and creating a movement had the potential to instill a deeper level of commitment from my team members.

I put four categories on the board: *Us, Clients, Local,* and *Global.* Without any preemptive framing, I invited our team members to sign up under one that they felt called to. Did they want to multiply the efforts for us and take better care of our team? Did they want to multiply the efforts for our clients—which had nothing to do with adding more clients but was about doing more for the clients we already had by finding ways to show them even more gratitude? Did they want to multiply for our local community by pouring into those we live in proximity with—which wasn't just about donating money to charity but about finding movements we could create? Or, lastly, did they want to multiply for the biggest needs around the world?

Unplanned and unscripted, I invited everybody to come up to the board and write their name underneath the category they felt most called to. People divided themselves up naturally—simply by what was in their gut. That was an inkling for me: we were onto something special. After they signed up, I announced that I was going to give $10,000 of my own money to each of the four groups. Their challenge was to multiply it. They didn't necessarily have to multiply the money; they needed to multiply the impact.

I specified that I wanted the people who were in traditional leadership roles at our company to *not* be the leaders of their groups. I didn't want our leaders to be in that same position because this was not only an effort to multiply the good we were doing in the world, it was also an effort to multiply leadership and opportunity for our team members. I realized that what we were doing was massively contagious. By talking about making a difference, by talking about transformation not transactions, our team lined up in droves.

Of course, everything is contagious, so if we focus on transactions and dollars alone, that's what other folks in our world will focus on too. With the four multiply groups, we were intentional in curating an environment where those who were the most generous were contagious for everyone else. This infected our environment in the most positive way. I saw people who weren't necessarily givers to begin with, or had never been shown the way in the past, work for one of our multiply groups and change the way they showed up every day, both in their personal lives and the impact they had on the world.

MULTIPLY GROUPS ACHIEVE RESULTS

We asked the groups to report back in one month. The first group to respond was the Multiply Us group. They had two parts to their presentation. The first action they took was providing healthy snacks available for purchase in the lunchroom. I sat there with encouragement for their efforts but also disappointment. Was my $10,000 going toward *snacks*? I wondered what I had gotten myself into.

But their presentation quickly changed my initial reaction. They explained that providing healthy snacks was the immediate, surface-level contribution they could make. Team members were often making bad, impulsive food decisions because there were no healthy options available. Following that, the second part of their presentation really opened my eyes. They had pooled together some of the $10,000, as well as cash from other team members, and created a real estate investment group. Two members of the Multiply Us group had previously been wealth managers in the finance world, and they jumped on this investment opportunity. They invested in real estate, cybercurrency, and other ventures that looked advantageous.

The result was astounding. With their strategic efforts, the $10,000 of seed money will turn into over $1 million of value through retirement accounts, real estate investing, and strategic partnerships. By the time the Multiply Us group had finished their presentation, my jaw was on the floor. I realized that sometimes people just needed permission—I just needed to say, "Go and do," giving them permission to be creative. With that, they created something I never could have created on my own.

The Multiply Clients group merged with our events coordinator to ramp up the energy that we put into client events. Our client events are one of the main ways we take great care of those we love the most, and the Multiply Clients group multiplied these efforts: we now do eight events throughout the year ranging from 100 families to 1,500 households engaged for a single event. We give clients date-night packages and host improv comedy nights. We reach out to them in other ways, too, with parties in our office parking lot, free pies a few days before Thanksgiving, and invitations to do community service together.

The Multiply Local group decided to partner with the United Way to put on a gala to raise money and awareness. In its inaugural year, having used only a few thousand of the $10,000 in seed money, they raised over $20,000.

The final group, Multiply Global, has provided a vital resource for those in need by building wells in third-world countries where clean water is a massive issue. In addition, we've sent three groups overseas to do mission work and have plans to do many more trips. The efforts and ripples created by this group are being felt around the world.

All of these group successes happened simply by giving our team members permission to show up and do good. When you open your life to do things for other people, your life becomes expansive and unlimited—and your efforts get multiplied.

When you open your life to do things for other people, your life becomes expansive and unlimited—and your efforts get multiplied.

PLAY FOR THE PERSON NEXT TO US

My alma mater is North Dakota State University, and the NDSU Bison football team has won seven of the last eight national championships in the FCS division of college football. It's one of the most storied programs in the history of college sports. I'm a huge Bison fan. As I've followed this team, I've sat sixth row at the thirty-yard line for every home game, I've traveled across the country to watch their games, and I've tailgated five hours the morning of each home game—you know, for the team. Through the journey, I've paid very close attention to how they operate as champions. They have a TV show on Sunday mornings where the coach and some players are interviewed. When asked, "What does it mean to be a Bison?" or "What does Bison pride mean to you?" what I hear the players say in almost every single interview is this: "I've learned to play for the person next to me."

I've been enamored with that saying because it recognizes that real champions are multipliers. The NDSU Bison don't have names on the backs of their jerseys. It's about the team name on the front. Real champions are playing for the person(s) next to them, not to boast their own individual accomplishments.

If I do something great, that's a great thing for me. But my playing small does not serve the world. (I got this idea from Marianne Williamson's poem "Our Deepest Fear"—*Your playing small / Does not serve the world*—and I'll return to this inspiring poem later in the book.) If I can be contagious enough for somebody else to catch on, then a real movement starts to happen. My playing is not meant for me; it's meant for the person next to me.

"YOU'RE NOT THAT IMPORTANT"

Understanding that good works are set aside for us to do and that multiplying our efforts is how we make a real impact means we must recognize that each of us, individually, is *just not all that important*. Thinking that you are the foundation of keeping something together is a dangerous path to walk. I learned this from my mentor Rollie when I was in college, yet I've still made the mistake far too many times of thinking that I am of crazy importance. I need to keep reminding myself.

A few months after my mom died, I was sharing with Rollie how I felt so overwhelmed. I was vice president of my fraternity, vice president of the entire student body, working twenty hours per week at a local restaurant, and taking a full course load of credits. But I was the most broken I had ever been in my life because I had just lost my only parent.

Rollie looked at me with love and care, and he said, "Erik, I hate to tell you this, but you're not that important." It was some of the truest and most honest feedback I've ever received. So a word of caution to my readers: yes, we have the possibility to multiply, but we aren't the power source. We're the extension cord. When we are connected to the right people and the right motivations, amazing things can happen through us. But we, our individual selves, carry very little power—like an extension cord without a power source. We should not believe that we are the most powerful force in this equation. We're not. However, when we're acting as an extension cord and are connected to the right things, then greatness can and will happen through us.

> *We're the extension cord. When we are connected to the right people and the right motivations, amazing things can happen through us.*

SELL A HOME, SAVE A CHILD

After my time in Haiti, God had put it in my heart to start an orphanage. It was a bizarre thing to desire, and yet I couldn't shake it. Years went by, and the idea only grew stronger. I had to do something big with my life and this new wealth I was making.

I caught wind of a Realtor out of Portland, Oregon, that was using his real estate business to help support a children's home in Nicaragua. And when I first met Nick Shivers, I was starstruck. He was one of the country's top Realtors and seemed larger than life to me. I asked him out to lunch as we were both attending a real estate convention in Austin, Texas, as I had to understand how to do all this.

I had researched the fundamental steps of starting an orphanage and was overwhelmed with how difficult this was going to be. Yet as Nick and I broke bread together over lunch, I realized that Nick had it figured out by partnering with an already existing organization. He was using his real estate business to help rescue kids from some of the most ungodly situations imaginable. The Villa Esperanza in Nicaragua was rescuing young girls from the local garbage dump where they would line up to do unspeakable things with the garbage truck drivers—just so their family would have first pick at the dump.

Nick had partnered with Forward Edge International, a nonprofit based out of Vancouver, Washington, that is actively helping to rescue kids and give them life all over the world. He shared with me his purpose—and that is to serve people and save kids, all through selling real estate.

Over that lunch I realized that God had brought us together to multiply good throughout the world. And as our friendship bloomed over the next couple of years, we kept talking about what to do together. Nothing immediately clicked—that is, until I found myself at a Casting Crowns concert. The lead singer, Mark Hall, gave a sermonette in the middle of their show about how we aren't called to sit on the sidelines. Our call and command is to get in the arena and get our hands dirty.

I was on fire—and I quickly called Nick. My wife, Emily, and I took a trip out to Portland a couple of weeks later so we could activate

> *Our call and command is to get in the arena and get our hands dirty.*

something with Nick. We knew we wanted our businesses to have massive purpose, and we knew we couldn't be the only ones. Thus, we birthed the Sell a Home, Save a Child (SAHSAC) movement. In its simplest form, the SAHSAC movement empowers Realtors and partners around the country to use their businesses as a way to do good in this world. Together we can rescue kids and make a forever difference in someone's life. Together we do well to do good.

Every team member at Hatch Realty donates a portion of their commission to SAHSAC. We take mission trips annually in partnership with other Realtors and vendors around the country who are passionate about kids. SAHSAC has etched itself onto the hearts of our team members, many of our clients, and prayerfully those kids that have a better chance at life now because of a crazy idea by Nick and me.

This movement helps us to attract people with the same heartbeat as us—both clients and team members. This movement helps to protect our commissions from being negotiated. This movement has helped us to close deals with potential clients. This movement has made a profound impact on the lives of our team members and those we have the privilege of serving. This movement is multiplying in action.

In the last four or so years, we have raised over $1.3 million to help save kids all around the globe. And we're just getting started. To learn more, go to sellahomesaveachild.org.

ME BECOMES *WE*

When I started my first real estate team, we had what appeared to be immediate success—yet it was anything but. I was the person who had massive amounts of sales, and everybody else was left grinding and working their tails off just to try to gain some traction and some momentum. I was working for me, and I had other people working for me as well. The key word was *me*. It was me, me, me.

After getting kicked out of that brokerage, I turned *me* upside down. When you do that, *me* becomes *we*. *We* made the change of how *we* led, and I made the change in how I poured into people. Instead of them pouring into me, I poured into them. Huge amounts of success were a by-product of that. My team members were changing their stars and becoming extremely successful. And there was plenty of success left for me too.

My leadership cascaded down and multiplied through the way these folks' lives were being impacted. I opened my life up to serve other people; from there, my life became more expansive, even unlimited. I had possibilities bestowed upon me that I had never thought were possible. I had invitations into people's lives and worlds I had never expected.

As somebody who did it the wrong way, I can say with confidence that showing up to do good works and play for the person next to you is the clearest, most expansive way to multiply your efforts. And for that multiplying to really take off, you need an environment that's contagious, which starts with changing your mindset and giving your team members permission to be their full selves in their workplace.

CHAPTER 3

CHANGE YOUR MINDSET

Popular culture says our work lives and home lives should never intersect. The message is that you shouldn't bring your personal business to the office. But as I developed a passion for the work that I did and as challenging things came up in my personal life, it was nearly impossible to leave work at work and home at home. Over the five-year period that my wife and I battled infertility, there was just no way to keep my home life separate and stay sane. I went through periods of being open about it and periods of being completely closed off. It's so clear which of those two allows you to be your full self and a more productive team member—and to have a more fulfilling life.

From the first moments after Emily and I got married, people at the church started asking us when we were going to have kids. We were pressured from the congregation, the youth group, everyone. The questions were both flattering and annoying. We didn't want to have children right away, but after a few years, we were ready. Then infertility became our norm. Because I had close relationships at the church, I could talk with coworkers and my youth group kids about what Emily and I were dealing with.

My work at the church was rooted in the concept of relational ministry. People trusted me when we had a relationship established. It's a servant model that I subscribed to with my youth group. I had great relationships with them; we would talk about the high highs and low lows. Through round after round of IUI, the people I was closest with at the church—members of the congregation, my coworkers, and the kids in my youth group—knew that Emily and I wanted to be parents and that we were struggling.

But when I moved into real estate, I was transplanted into a different environment, and I changed the way I created community. I abandoned the idea of relational ministry. I held things back; I wasn't talking with anyone at work (outside of a select few) about our experience trying to have a baby. This was an obscenely tough battle for me—holding in all that pain and guilt and shame that can be associated with something like infertility. I had abandoned being fully transparent with people because I was now in a for-profit, formal role. When I moved to the professional world, I thought I had to change. I did, I closed up, and I was miserable.

After IUI didn't work, we switched to IVF and went through three miscarriages and one ectopic pregnancy, which required surgery, before our last embryo turned into our daughter, Finley. It was easy to talk about infertility once we were through it. Yet it was only when I was at the church, surrounded by a community that was rooted in deep relationships, that I was talking about what was really going on in my life.

WORK AGAINST THE GRAIN
OF POPULAR CULTURE

As we built Hatch Realty, I knew I wanted to create a community more like my youth group. I didn't want what popular culture told me a workplace should be. I wanted a place where we talked about the high highs and low lows. Instead of valuing what was easy, instead of quick transactions, we needed to go deeper and be more intentional with each other. We started approaching business with the understanding that our environment was one of embracing one another in our fullness, not excluding parts of ourselves. To do this, we had to go against what people traditionally feel is a business-type environment in a business setting.

Instead of valuing what was easy, instead of quick transactions, we needed to go deeper and be more intentional with each other.

As the company grew, I realized that what I was doing wasn't a job, and it wasn't even a career—it was a lifestyle, one in which I was transparent and open and connected with those who were within my world. They knew my good days, and they knew my bad days. I didn't hide from that.

I'm convinced that throughout this country there are tens of millions of people just like me—in real estate and health care and education and nonprofits and for-profits and everywhere in between—who are craving connection. They are deeply broken on the inside, and when they arrive at work, they have to compartmentalize their brokenness. They're not given permission in the workplace to talk about what's really going on in their lives. They're not given the opportunity to be their true selves. Instead they have to be a different version of themselves, which eats up their energy and capabilities.

I'd love to tell you that everyone in my companies trusts their fellow team members with all their junk. That just isn't the truth. As I write this, some of my work family is struggling with massive battles, and they aren't talking about it. It is insanely hard to open up. We see all the symptoms yet fail to understand what the ailment is. Most everyone knows they are battling something heavy—and we're rendered helpless without that person opening up.

It takes true strength and trust to be vulnerable. The strongest people I know are those that show how weak they are.

When illness or struggle shows up in someone's life, it's met with this idea that you cannot have cancer at work. You cannot have infertility issues in the workplace. But our home life naturally intersects with our work life. It's all interconnected. How could I have kept the infertility issues that Emily and I were facing separate and still show up as my full self to work every day? I couldn't. I was closed up and miserable. Hiding something big does not allow anyone to be their full self.

Contemporary thinking values being quick and easy rather than satisfying. But if we want to succeed in business and life, instead of faster, better, and more, we need to be slower, deeper, and more intentional. Transparency actually allows you to grow faster because you build trust so quickly. The ironic thing about slowing down is that it actually gives you permission to speed up. The deeper you go, the higher you can build. The more you know about a team member, the more able you are to help that person become their best self.

When it comes to building our teams and building up our team members, we need to slow down, go deeper, and uncover things that haven't been dealt with in the past. This starts with the interview process.

"I'M NOT GOING TO CRY FOR YOU"

If people want to work with us, one of the precursors is that they have to be willing to be vulnerable. In chapter 1, I wrote about the group mentality on display when people come into our world and how this starts with the first time they step into our organization. We hold a career night prior to interviewing a single candidate. This is uncommon in most industries, but it serves an important purpose, allowing us to see the whites of their eyes and understand the energy they bring rather than trying to figure that out with a résumé.

During career night, we tell them about our nine-step hiring process. (These steps are covered in full in chapter 7.) The seventh step is inviting them to be part of a three-hour interview. More details are shared in that interview than in any of the other eight steps. During the first ninety minutes, we don't ask anything about work. We ask for the person's life story. We want to know the high highs and the low lows of their life. In fact we get to work details only in the last thirty minutes or so. When we do get to that point, we don't say things like, "Tell me a time you were managed well." Instead we say, "Tell us about what gives you life and makes you come alive." We try to find out what they're passionate about rather than asking questions that prompt rehearsed answers.

Throughout those first ninety minutes, we are learning about someone's life story and are able to start peeling back that onion to see all the different things they can provide. We all have our scripts that we reiterate again and again, so our goal is to get people out of routinized answers. During career night, when I tell applicants about the three-hour interview, I tell them that sometimes we stumble upon emotions that are a little raw. We want to see people open up and trust us with their transparency and vulnerability. Believe it or not, in most of our interviews, when done right, people will cry or at least get choked up because they're talking about deep things they maybe haven't tended to. That allows us to see how they respond, to see their resilience, and to see the baggage and opportunities they bring with them.

During one interview, I was going deeper than what the candidate was comfortable with. She said, "Listen, I'm not going to cry for you." It stopped me dead in my tracks, and I realized that she didn't fit in our workplace because she wasn't willing to be vulnerable. Most businesses don't ask for vulnerability. In fact most other businesses say vulnerability is a bad thing. I certainly didn't need her to cry for me—that was not the goal—but I did need her to show up and show some trust and vulnerability. She wasn't willing to do that.

We built a business based on people being open books and being accepted, warts and all, rather than people having to put on their Sunday best to come to work and act like everything is okay when really, sometimes, it just isn't. The speed of trust for us versus most other businesses is so much greater because we make connections that go way past the surface.

THE OAK TREE MINDSET

I recently spoke at Microsoft, which has its second-largest campus in the US in Fargo. They asked me to talk about leadership, and I took them through an exercise called the Oak Tree. I learned this exercise at Camp Metigoshe, where I was a camp counselor for two summers while in college.

At the camp we gathered in the middle of a field. On one side was an oak tree, and on the other side was a barren field. Before we dove in, we set some boundaries: we told everyone that there's always a safe side where you can blend in and not stand out, and they always have permission to do that if they choose.

The game worked like this: when a statement was made, we were all given the option of going to the oak tree. It starts with a statement like "If you're a coffee drinker, go to the oak tree." You can't stand in the middle as someone who's neutral; you have to pick a side and say, "Yes, I'm a coffee drinker" or "No, I'm not a coffee drinker." That line is drawn, and you're able to see what community you find yourself in. The next statements are equally low stakes:

"If you prefer the toilet paper to hang under instead of over, go to the oak tree."

"If you had braces in high school, go to the oak tree."

"If you've ever split your pants in public, go to the oak tree."

You start with things that get people laughing and comfortable, and you start to see that there are differences and similarities with all of us.

Then we start getting a little deeper. With this we're calling people to be a little more courageous; we're inviting them to unveil some layers of their onion that maybe they haven't unveiled before in the company of other people. We think this is how relationships are really built within the workplace and our lives. These questions usually revolve around upbringing:

"If you were an only child, go to the oak tree."

"If you were raised in a single-parent home, go to the oak tree."

These are still mostly safe, mostly surface-level questions. Then we start saying things along the following lines:

"If you battled major insecurities growing up, go to the oak tree."

"If, when you look in the mirror, you don't like what's reflected back and you see the negative before the positive, go the oak tree."

Now, just when they think, "Okay, I understand what we're doing here," we go really deep. At this point we remind them that they can stay safe and encourage them to do that if they'd like to. But everything is contagious, and we usually find that this process creates a contagious confidence to stand out and be different that really starts to show itself. We say things along the following lines:

"If you have ever experienced abuse of any kind, go to the oak tree."

"If you or any of your immediate family members battle any sort of addiction, go to the oak tree."

We see people who aren't afraid to go to the oak tree because we've created an environment that says being different is exalted rather than condemned. Everyone has a deeper story, and we can't take people at surface level. We see strength arise, and the encouragement from this exercise allows people to feel like they have learned an awful lot about each other.

BUILDING BETTER BEHAVIORS AND HABITS

Connecting deeply with people is learned over time. Before it shows up naturally, you need to practice it, which means continuously encouraging transparency and vulnerability. We want relationships to happen quickly, but to actually build a relationship and truly connect with people takes an arduous amount of time and effort. We have to practice this intentionally.

This is a very different mindset from how we tend to show up at the office. We take people at surface level based on who they say they are and our impression of them. But when do we take the time to really understand what's ticking inside of them? The oak tree exercise provides a framework for people to connect and understand the intricacies, the beauty, and the vivid colors of people's lives.

This has nothing to do with selling real estate or making money—it has everything to do with building trust and rapport within a workplace. We do this deeper-level work on a regular basis within Hatch Realty and Hatch Coaching. Continually stressing transparency allows our teams to trust each other more. Our team members show up to a place that feels like a warm embrace rather than a cold welcome. When people can be transparent and trust each other, they tend to be able to be less fake. And when people are less fake, they're not exhausting themselves trying to compartmentalize. Others are able to receive them more, and the amount of work they do is substantially higher because we're giving them space and permission to be their authentic selves.

Our team members show up to a place that feels like a warm embrace rather than a cold welcome.

This kind of workplace environment is also a retention tool. Having not been forced to fake it until they make it, they're going to work harder for the people who have their back. They're going to have more passion for the company because the company is working for them instead of them working for the company. When problems do arise, because we have cultivated the courage to be transparent and everybody is no longer hiding their own baggage, they're going to have the courage to speak up. When something isn't right, you've already given permission to talk about the things that aren't roses and rainbows. When people see progression in the workplace because they've shown up as contributors, when people have trusted us enough to allow for healing to happen in their hearts, that individual is going to be a more successful team member and part of a more inclusive community.

This can't just happen once or twice. You must instill in your organization a culture where vulnerability and connection becomes the everyday norm. Leadership has everything to do with influence and little to do with title or power. Most people are sitting back in the workplace expecting the other guy to do it, but we all have the ability to influence and impact the world around us. For every person who finds themselves working with other people, the charge is to embrace transparency, encourage people to unveil things in their lives that haven't been talked about at work, and build an organization that handles more than just transactions. Do that and watch how quickly trust is built.

When people trust one another, I believe that everything gets easier. Teams rally together without hesitation. Problems get solved faster because there's less second-guessing of one another. Relationships are built on a sturdier foundation that goes beyond the surface level. Team members begin to instill more trust in their leader. And production and performance increase drastically—all because people trust each other more.

HOW WE TREAT PEOPLE MATTERS

As I've grown as a leader, I've found that people are anything but expendable. Your behavior determines your culture, and how we treat people matters deeply. Team members notice when people are treated as expendable or if they get away with murder. Leaders make bold statements through their actions.

I've heard this adage my entire life: "Slow to hire, quick to fire." Frankly I hate it. I think it's a terrible way to treat people. I believe that "slow to hire" is 100 percent correct, but I would rephrase the second part as "quick to love." If we're going to invest in someone who has uprooted their life to come work with us in our culture, then when they're struggling, we're going to run toward them instead of running away.

As business owners and leaders, we have the responsibility to help that person get better, not just when we hire them but every moment of every day. Now, let me put an asterisk on this: if a team member is making serious choices to fall away from the core of the business and your culture, then they should no longer be a part of your organization. Grace is sometimes given when someone falls out of culture, but you must have a strong enough hold on your business to protect the whole before the individual.

When someone on your team is struggling—they've fallen short; life is happening to them, and they're not their best self—they are typically put on a performance improvement plan or PIP. Most of the time, in a traditional business setting, these PIPs don't work. I've read studies that show 80–90 percent of people who are put on PIPs don't actually improve.

I believe that PIPs fail when they are assigned rather than being collaborative. Our team members have far more buy-in when it's something they have their fingerprints on rather than something that's handed down to them. PIPs should be embraced by both the individual falling short and their leader or supervisor. These improvement plans should not just be assigned to someone who is struggling with the expectation that they will magically turn things around on their own. We need to support people in turning things around; it's not just going to magically happen. The PIP is both for the supervisor and the person that's struggling. It's all hands on deck!

Early in the book, I mentioned the Homeless and Hungry Movement, which my youth group kids and I created together. The old idea around solving homelessness and poverty was encouraging someone who is homeless to get their addiction or mental health issues under control and get a job, then give them the housing. Today a massive movement is changing this idea. The "housing first" model says, "We're going to give you housing so you can get whatever you're dealing with under control, whether it's addiction or mental health issues or trauma. Then you can get a job." This model has proven to be a much better way of getting someone out of the poverty cycle.

The core idea behind the housing first model is simply putting someone in a better position to be able to succeed. On our teams, we need to help people succeed on a more easily attainable level by changing the way we approach them. We do so by loving them where they're at and devising an improvement plan *with* them—where they have decided, "I want to get better, and here are the things I'm going to do"—rather than dictating a PIP *to* them. We help with the root cause by peeling back the layers and working to understand what is ticking inside of them. Then we tend to those issues alongside them.

We can't abandon people in their tough times and simply hope that they're going to get better. Hope is a great thing to have but a terrible business strategy. I'm convinced that the correct business strategy is to run toward them like a firefighter, to come alongside them and help with the tough things that are going on in their life and their business. It's a much slower process—because you, as the leader, have to show up more—but when we run toward our struggling team members rather than assign a PIP and run away, improvement has a much greater likelihood of happening.

We cannot expect someone to go from struggling to achieving in a day. Instead we monitor the crescendo, looking for gradual improvement, and we do so not by assigning them tasks to do on their own but by walking right there alongside them. This takes more time in the beginning but far less time than firing someone and going through the hiring process and the trust-building process all over again. Plus I don't believe people should be treated as expendable. The result of working with your team in this way is less money spent, deeper relationships, and higher retention. Our job is to be slow to hire and quick to love.

> *We cannot expect someone to go from struggling to achieving in a day.*

*   *   *

Changing your mindset means embracing a workplace that allows people to talk about what's really going on in their lives. It means creating a contagiously transparent environment in which people are encouraged to be their full selves. It means running toward your team members who are struggling. With that kind of mindset, you're starting to build a rock-solid foundation for your business.

CHAPTER 4

THE IMPORTANCE OF FOUNDATION

After I presented at an entrepreneurial class at North Dakota State University, a few students reached out to me. They wanted advice on how to be an entrepreneur and how to get involved in real estate. One of the rules I adhere to whenever somebody I haven't met wants to meet with me is I put up a couple of obstacles to see if they're serious. I did that for these students—by telling them I was busy and could reconnect with them at a later date. Like almost always happens, most of them didn't respond after being faced with the slightest barrier. But one student was diligent. She reached out to me again and asked for a meeting.

Her poise, demeanor, and energy—and the questions she asked—were fascinating to me. I learned she had started NDSU at the age of sixteen and would soon be graduating at nineteen. She was trying to figure out what was next. My hope is that she circles back and we get the chance to have her as one of our team members. At this point I don't know the end of that story, but I want to share what we talked about because it led me to this idea of *foundation*.

She asked me how I became an entrepreneur and about the things I was passionate about—the things that fill my heart with joy, those situations and relationships that bring energy rather than suck the life out of us. Then she asked a simple question: "Why real estate?" I paused and really took some time to figure out how to answer.

Truthfully I don't care much about real estate. The brick and mortar never really mattered to me. The people inside the properties, however, those were the folks I cared about. I told her that as I grew and scaled the business, I found myself working with hundreds of clients. I felt like I was doing a hit-and-run job. I worked on maintaining relationships through social media and client events, but I felt like I was a lot to them for a little period of time. My desire was to be a lot for a long period of time.

I didn't have a clear answer to her "Why real estate?" question. Real estate wasn't my passion; people were my passion. It was her poignant questions that led me to this idea of foundation. My foundation was leadership, creativity, relationships, and service. Those things gave me joy and helped me to feel like I was living with purpose. I told her, "Real estate is simply the means by which I can lead a fulfilling life."

SITUATIONAL IDENTITY CRISIS

Last chapter I talked about how compartmentalizing ourselves at work harms our energy and capability. Part of foundation is being in alignment with one's purpose in life. Abandoning the purpose of who we are and being a different version of ourselves for eight or ten or twelve hours a day is idiotic. Instead, aligning those together—so people can be passionate about who they are in life and continue like that in the workplace—has been freeing in our environment.

Abandoning the purpose of who we are and being a different version of ourselves for eight or ten or twelve hours a day is idiotic.

One of my favorite speakers and authors is a pastor from Mosaic Church in Hollywood, California, named Erwin McManus. In one of his sermons, he talks about situational identity crisis. This refers to how, in different situations, we often struggle because we're trying to remember who we're supposed to be. For example, when you go to church, you're supposed to put on your Sunday best. When you go to an athletic field, you're supposed to be your aggressive self. When you're working with children or the elderly, you're supposed to be nurturing, soft, and caring. When you're in the business world, you're supposed to be cutthroat, ruthless, and relentless.

Furthermore, many businesses want us to be buttoned-up employees who don't bring any baggage with them to the workplace. Leave your depression at the door. Don't even think about allowing your family struggles to show their ugly face at the office. Keep your personal life out of your professional life.

It's really difficult to be anything close to our full selves when we're trying to figure out who we're supposed to be at any given time. If I'm being true to my foundation, I can build whatever infrastructure I want and shouldn't have to be somebody different in each situation. I need and want to be the same passionate person I am for my faith with my family and the people I work with. If I really want a fulfilling life, I shouldn't have to wear a mask when I step into different environments.

The challenge remains for those of us who are stuck in jobs that don't allow us to be our true selves or who are stuck in relationships where we're not given the ability to shine. Because we're all meant to shine—we're all meant to bring warmth and light to this world. When you're in line with who you're really meant to be, the light you have inside of you becomes completely intoxicating for others. I believe that people want to have a life that's full of purpose, and we want to have careers where we're not dealing with situational identity crises and having to hang up our life's passions from nine-to-five.

Merging these together have helped me create a foundation at Hatch Realty and Hatch Coaching that has been masterfully infectious. This is not something that can be learned; it's something that you have if you've been intentional about building it. We have to possess knowledge and be experts in our fields, of course, but that can be learned. Skills are learned, while foundations are built by allowing people to be their full selves. In our world, allowing for every team member's purpose to be part of our foundation has created that infectious environment.

> *Skills are learned, while foundations are built by allowing people to be their full selves.*

FOUNDATIONS: ENVIRONMENT, CHARACTER, CULTURE

Relational is foundational. Many organizations make decisions about their foundation based on numbers, but real foundational pieces are environment, character, and culture. The real estate business is about people, not the products that we sell. Although the only thing you'll find in my toolbox is my checkbook, I do know the importance of a strong foundation that is based on specific needs and is permeable to change. Foundations—whether literal (the foundation of a house) or figurative (the foundation of your business)—should be suited for the specific environment and people. The way you incorporate these elements to go deep with the foundation, so you can ultimately build higher, is to pay attention to the environment you're in, the character you bleed out from every pore, and the culture and the heartbeat you're creating within your organization.

Environment

In real estate we talk about foundations all the time. If you're building a house in Fargo, North Dakota, the foundation looks very different than if you're building a house in Phoenix, Arizona. In Fargo our soil is clay, which is ridiculously impermeable and unstable. We're also in a floodplain. We have to go really deep for our foundations, and we have to floodproof the basement. (The three little pigs would be foolish to build their house in Fargo.) If you're building a house in Phoenix, however, your foundation calls for something totally different. You have to pay attention to 120-degree heat. Fargo has 50 below weather, terrible soil, and floods. The foundations we build are completely dependent on the environment in which we find ourselves.

Let's look at the kinds of environments people get to work in at Hatch Realty and how that determines their foundations. Our team members are either fully salaried, partially salaried and partially compensated with commission, or full commission. Each one requires a different foundation—a different level of risk and reward. Yet there are so many similarities that we must pay attention to as well. All great foundations are malleable; they are able to mold and move. Business infrastructures that are impermeable to change crumble all the time, and it's rarely because of economic conditions (although that does play a factor every once in a while). The number of businesses being started today is higher than it's ever been, and the number of businesses not making it and collapsing is also higher than it's ever been. So many businesses are rooted in the wrong kind of foundation. They are incorrectly built based on their environment.

Many business owners pay more attention to things like profit-and-loss statements than they do growing relationships with the people who work in the building. Their infrastructure is built on things that make sense to them—the things that are black and white, the things that are easily explained and understood. For business leaders who are used to things being black and white, dealing with the emotions and deeper layers that people bring to the workplace can result in a Rubik's Cube of confusion.

But most of life happens outside of work. And when folks come to work, they're encouraged to fit into a box. If a foundation is going to be sturdy, boxes shouldn't be a part of it. A sturdy foundation does not force its people into situational identity crises. The way concrete mixes and settles is that all the different elements merge together, which is followed by time to harden. That's how a foundation stays strong. We then have to pay very close attention to what is built on top of it.

Quite often people build a foundation for something in their life as shallow as possible so they can quickly get to building something on top of it. Think of a romantic relationship. If the foundation of your relationship is drinking or partying, you can only build so high. If the foundation of your relationship is sex, you can only build so high. But if your foundation is to be built so that you can see how high you can truly go, it's going to require digging much deeper and it's going to take longer for that foundation to settle and set.

Character

Character is something that shows itself when people aren't looking. In my younger years, I learned from my mother that character was also doing the things that future Erik would thank me for rather than allowing Erik of yesterday to hold me back. Still, to this day, my character struggles. My thoughts get the best of me, and sometimes I act in ways that I shouldn't. But that's the thing: we all have darkness inside of us. We all have the opportunity to define our character when nobody is watching. We all have that character piece that's foundational.

When we opened up Hatch Realty in 2014, we landed at our very first office—an old pediatric dentist office built in the 1950s. Doing my due diligence, I hired an inspector to look deeper into the property, and he brought me down to the basement to investigate a large crack in the foundation. He said to me, "Erik, I don't know if this foundation moved or is moving. You need to keep an eye on it." As we all have cracks from mistakes of the past, and we still struggle daily to keep our character intact, it's imperative that we watch our foundations closely. Are the cracks in our foundations happening right now, from current missteps, or are they from the past? The cracks from yesterday may not be active, yet undue pressures can lead to major issues down the road.

We need to pay very close attention to the cracks that are there. Cracks don't mean that the house is going to come crumbling down, but they do mean we have to keep an eye on them. We have to keep an eye on the connecting pieces that we have with folks in our organization and what's going on in their lives. If cancer shows up, literal or figurative, for any of our team members, that crack can spread overnight. It's our call as leaders, and especially as servant leaders, to show up to help take care of that crack.

But it's not our job to fill the crack (unless we have the power to do so). I struggle with that all the time—thinking I can go and fix things that have nothing to do with me. Back in my ministry days, I saw terrible things happen in people's lives. I saw plenty of great things, too, and everyday grind kinds of things. But I regularly saw things like death and suicide and cancer—things that are really tough to digest on a regular basis.

My job was not to fix those things, although sometimes I thought that it was. One of our congregants was a man named Jon who had battled homelessness for years. When I saw Jon, he reminded me of my father. He was broken by addiction and had a desire to be better but was so deep in it that he couldn't rid himself of it. I wanted to help him get better by tending to those cracks and fixing his foundation. Every time I tried to do that, I was left disappointed, exhausted, and frustrated.

Cracks in people's lives happen all the time. Our call is to come alongside those people who are dealing with cracks in their foundations. We don't have to say the right things; we don't have to offer any kind of solution. We simply offer support. Just come alongside the person because the greatest gift you can give someone is your presence.

Most of us are moving so fast in our workplaces that we fail to build our foundations in the right way. We fail to go deep; we go shallow instead. To go deep takes time, and it means we have to slow down on other things that appear to be moneymaking and more important. But if you're going to build a skyscraper of an organization and an infrastructure that is deep and solid enough to withstand any storm, you have to take the time to simply be present. You don't have to have the right things to say. You simply need to be there and be aligned with that person. The gift of your time and your presence strengthens foundations much more than your ability to fill cracks. If your character is that of love and support, that just might be the right medicine for the troubles your team members are struggling with.

Culture

I remember the day I bought the ping-pong table for our office. I had this vision of office ping-pong tournaments—laughing like I was in a Bud Light commercial, our team members bonding left and right. What ended up happening was a couple of people played every once in a while. I don't think I've played more than one game in five years. Clearly it wasn't the epicenter of office culture that I expected it to be.

When we moved offices, that changed. I initially thought a ping-pong table would signify our culture. Eventually it did become a part of our culture—but not in the way I expected. Today the ping-pong table resides in our break room, where people can be found making lunch, hanging out, and having casual conversations. Maybe they just finished up in the massage chair or on the exercise bike and then went and played a game of ping-pong. Above the ping-pong table is a TV with cable where people watch sporting events, soap operas, or whatever else they choose.

Our culture is so loosey goosey that no one punches a clock. Nobody is required to check in or out; everyone just has a job that they're expected to do. As we have developed culture this way, even giving people unlimited time off, I wanted the ping-pong table to be the signifying piece that said, "We play a lot. We let our hair down. We're the cool place to work." Having a ping-pong table is all well and good, and playing a game after you've worked hard is just fine. But culture is not having a ping-pong table, team meals, or going to happy hours. Those are signs of culture. Your culture is how you treat one another.

> ## Your culture is how you treat one another.

I talked about how our foundations need to go deep. There's nothing deep about a ping-pong table or a happy hour. But there is something deep about going and connecting with someone you love and trust over a game of ping-pong or drinks after work. Those activities look a lot different when your relationships aren't surface level.

In the end I don't like the word *culture* all that much. At this point, it's become very watered down. I see businesses all over talk about how they have great cultures: "We have a work hard, play hard culture" is a common line. Those with a ping-pong table are saying something like, "I care about this culture and want people to be able to let their hair down and play."

I don't think that the word *culture* and how it's typically used signifies what we're really saying. I think we're talking more about the heartbeat of the organization. The heartbeat that matters is the way we're showing up in the lives of the people we're connected with. It's the ability to peel back the layers of the onion and get connected with those folks through the speed of trust, which comes through vulnerability and connection. That's the kind of culture that I crave.

SUBCULTURES AND SIDE HUSTLES

A critical part of culture is figuring out side projects that people are passionate about. In the show *The Office*, there's a party-planning committee. There's dysfunction, of course, which makes it hilarious and awkward, but this party-planning committee is a good example of a subculture. They have the commonality of throwing parties together. Culture is meant to incorporate the entire organization, but realistically, our worlds are filled with subcultures. Subcultures—or side hustles, as we sometimes call them—are so important.

Subcultures can be breeding grounds for either massive positivity or destruction. The positivity comes when you're aligning forces and building things together. The multiply groups I talked about in chapter 2 are examples of positive side hustles. The destruction comes when they turn into pockets of gossip, negativity, or complaint. If we're going to own our subcultures by leaning into them and supporting them, we need to pay attention to exactly how layered our cultures are and where opportunities arise for our team members to pursue side hustles.

Having subcultures and side hustles is an important way for you to continue to pour into your organization and allow for autonomy and freedom and creativity and growth. People hit glass ceilings in a regular culture because often their jobs don't allow them to be their best selves. Yet opportunities arise within our workplaces to create these subcultures that give people permission to shine. A great culture pulls out of people what's inside of them, helping them to be their best selves. You can't buy culture, and you can't simply provide items, like a ping-pong table, that replicate a great culture. Culture comes from the relationships you have and the time you invest in them. That's where trust is built. It also determines the speed in which you can build.

At Hatch Realty and Hatch Coaching, we continually find ways to go deep instead of just going along with surface-level conversations. Every ninety days, we do something called "quarterly pattern interrupts." We stop work for a day, everyone gets paid their full salary, and we spend the day connecting. We're giving team members a chance to connect with new people within the workplace so they're establishing new relationships. We're goofy, and we laugh, but we also do small-group time where people get really deep into what's going on in their lives, whether it be past, present, or future.

*　　*　　*

There's a song by the band Casting Crowns called "Slow Fade." It's about how most mistakes in life don't happen in the snap of a finger. Rather, it's a slow fade, a gradual deterioration of that foundation. Earthquakes do happen, of course, but most foundations fail because water permeates over many years. Most of us, however, tend to ignore these foundational issues; they happen out of sight, and it takes work to tend to them. But the problem is that this results in a slow fade. One day we recognize that it was a series of choices made over time that led to the deterioration of our organization.

The message of this chapter is to pay closer attention to your culture and the heartbeat of your organization. Everything in your environment needs to be harmonious. You need to make sure that leadership and team members are aligned in the same culture and priorities. Making sure everyone's priorities are in line, the subject of the next chapter, protects you from the slow fade that deteriorates so many businesses.

CHAPTER 5

PRIORITIES

If it's a purposeful life we crave, then taking care of ourselves must be a top priority. I've struggled with this. I've battled weight my entire life and haven't been consistent in making my health a priority. A low point came when I was twenty-one, after my mom passed away. It was a low point emotionally, but it was also a low point physically. When I decided to change my life and focus on my health for the first time, I made it a priority. That led me to losing sixty pounds and running a marathon.

But I've been inconsistent. After my marathon, over the next seven or eight years, I put that sixty pounds back on—along with another ten or twenty on top of it. Then in 2009 I prioritized my health again. I did ten months of P90X and Insanity. I played basketball five or six days a week. I had to shower three times a day because I was working out so much. I got into the best shape of my life and dropped seventy pounds in the process. I was in such good shape that I decided, spur of the moment, to run two half marathons. I just showed up and ran them because my physical fitness was so high. This all resulted from how I prioritized putting myself and my health first.

Then, yet again, I lost focus. This time it had to do with an injury: my hip had started to ail me, and I ended up having a hip replacement in my midthirties because it was so aggressively deteriorating from arthritis. I threw myself a decade-long pity party and stopped making my health a priority. I ate my feelings and barely exercised. And when I stepped on the scale, I was disgusted by what I saw: I was over one hundred pounds heavier than when I ran the marathon or when I did the stint with P90X and Insanity.

I know I can't be the only one who gets their priorities completely out of whack. I have other stories as well about not prioritizing my family or my team members—or about when I didn't focus on work like I needed to; I focused on transactions instead of leadership. I also have stories about times where my faith really stumbled. At those times my personal and professional development faltered because I had simply gotten comfortable and complacent in my faith and wasn't making it a priority. When things become comfortable, we often stop making them priorities.

When things become comfortable, we often stop making them priorities.

Tending to your priorities requires being intentional and consistent, two words we'll return to at the end of the chapter. I cannot emphasize enough the importance of priorities. I learned from my mom to put others before myself, which always sounds well and good, but the actual implementation of it is unbelievably dangerous. Having your priorities in order begins with tending to the base of your pyramid.

LEVEL 1: YOURSELF, YOUR FAMILY, YOUR FAITH

Having your priorities out of whack sometimes shows itself in literal ways (like gaining weight), but it can also show itself more subtly—in the things that go on in our minds, in the self-confidence that we have or lack, or in the certainty of the path that we're on. It can feel like you have it all as you pursue more clients, more transactions, and more money. But those things are empty promises that don't give you the deep satisfaction of caring for yourself, your family, and your faith. Without caring for your base, your ability to care for your team members, your clients, and your community is nearly impossible.

Self

When I got kicked out of my previous brokerage and was recovering from that, I made work the ultimate priority. It got all my focus and attention. But because work occupied so much of my focus, the other things in my life took a toll. In that one year of recovering from getting fired, when I prioritized work over everything else, I put on thirty pounds.

Having let my health fall by the wayside yet again, it was clear my priorities were out of whack. Today I'm back on track and hyper-focused. As I write this, I can say that I'm making my way back to a healthier lifestyle. I can't run anymore or play sports due to the hip replacement, so I'm hopping on an exercise bike almost every day. I'm also fueling my body in a healthy way by eating right. The idea of self-care, the first priority in your pyramid, is something often talked about yet rarely practiced.

Family

Over the three- or four-year period when I was building my real estate career, I worked ninety- to one-hundred-hour weeks every single week. As a Realtor, you can easily become a slave to your phone: every time the phone rang or a text or email came in, I jumped to that flashing light like it was the most important thing in the world. My wife was so understanding about taking a back seat because we were building our future together. She never made me feel guilty about it, but *I* felt guilty about it. I put my clients, other Realtors, and the pursuit of work as a higher priority than her.

Our families do not deserve our leftovers. They deserve the most energy and focus and time and love that we can give. Yet most of us, at the end of the day, simply give our families whatever we have left—*if* there's anything left in the tank. When my daughter, Finley, was born in 2014, I made the choice that everything was going to be different—that I was going to be more focused on family. I was going to be the better husband that my wife deserves. I was going to be the active father that I never had.

Today I can say with confidence that I am one hell of a father and one hell of a husband. It's

> *Our families do not deserve our leftovers.*

always been that way as a father, but it hasn't always been that way as a husband. I've fixed that. Now the only time I answer my phone when I'm in a conversation with someone is if it's my wife calling. Everyone else takes a back seat to her. She gets to interrupt everything else, and nothing interrupts her.

When I was working those ninety- to one-hundred-hour weeks, the consequences were that I didn't have time for much of anything else. I let go of many friendships I held dear for the pursuit of a bigger life. I don't say that with joy in my heart, but I'm also not apologetic about it—because I saw the bigger picture and knew the consequences that would come from it. There have been some very lonely days in my life, and I know the consequences of spending so many hours a week on my business. Today I have eighteen businesses that I have the fortune of investing in and being a part of (and hopefully many more to come). Because I spent thousands of hours invested in work, some pretty great consequences came from it.

If you're reading this, my guess is that you probably have a desire to have a bigger life. You're looking for more abundance, more love, more leadership, more wealth. These are common pursuits we share. A coach of mine, Shane Hipps, told me something that I can't get out of my mind. When evaluating choices, he talked about something different than right and wrong. With my two kids, we talk about right and wrong pretty frequently, but the language we use is different—it's the language that Shane emphasized. Instead of right and wrong, he said, we merely have choices and consequences. We simply need to understand the weight that goes into our decision making and the impact it will have.

For me, the most important partner I have in my life is my wife. Never do I make a decision about business or anything else without her input. We decide together. It's funny: I'm the author of this book when my wife should really be the one telling the story. Everything I have is because of her. Everything that I get the privilege of doing is supported by her. She is a brake to my gas pedal. At moments our dynamic makes me absolutely crazy, yet she has kept me from crashing into so many walls that I would have hit at one hundred miles per hour.

Faith

While you are not mandated by me or anyone else to have faith as something you pursue, I believe that working for something bigger and grander than you has so much value. When faith is part of your foundation, my feeling is that everything else can be built with much more ease. Most of us don't place a high enough priority on personal development, and for me personal development and faith go hand in hand.

My relationship with Jesus and my participation and involvement with the church are fundamental to who I am. I can't spend one hour a week at church and consider that a healthy commitment to my faith, at least by my standards. Similarly I can't work out for one hour a week or eat one salad for a meal once a week and say that I'm living a lifestyle that is worthy of pride and joy.

Faith has to be integrated for me—as something that shows itself in every fiber of our beings and all aspects of our lives. That means we need to be the same people of faith at home, at work, and with our friends as we are on Sunday mornings at church. We have the same priorities, the same concerns, the same desires. And then we have to continually fuel this engine. I'm talking about the books that we read, the conversations we have, the podcasts we listen to, and everything in between.

Earlier in my career, faith took up a large portion of my base. As a church youth pastor, I chose a lifestyle of devoting myself to faith and pouring into kids—doing whatever I could to make sure that they felt important, seen, and loved and that I could introduce them to Jesus. That took a plethora of time. We traveled around the world serving in every corner we could. I spent many nights and weekends investing in those kids. Often that meant time away from my wife. As a first-grade teacher, her job was from 7:30 a.m. to 3:00 p.m., and my nights and weekends were often consumed by my job. We made the decision together that we were going to make those sacrifices. It wasn't right or wrong; it was a series of choices and consequences.

It wasn't right or wrong; it was a series of choices and consequences.

If you're someone who is living a certain lifestyle to support one aspect of your life, you need to heavily weigh the consequences of each and every one of your decisions. Of course there are both positive and negative consequences. It's just a matter of what you're willing to live with and what your family is willing to live with.

LEVEL 2: TEAM MEMBERS

The second level of your pyramid is tending to your team members. If you're a solopreneur, or someone who doesn't have other people in your care, you could skip this level. However, if you have growth as any part of your design, then this level will start to matter eventually.

Most people in the real estate world who are developing teams get this level exceedingly wrong. A couple of years ago, I was talking with a Realtor friend of mine about business and connection. With great energy and confidence, he said, "You know what, Erik? Next year is the year I start putting my clients first." When he said it, I was dying a little bit on the inside. I believe that's a terrible model: If your clients come first, then your team gets the table scraps. Wouldn't you be much better off by first taking care of the servants—by serving those who have the clients in their watch—rather than skipping over them and hoping your team members merely survive the gauntlet that is your business?

Back in 2012 and 2013, before I got kicked out of my previous brokerage, I put my clients first—just like my Realtor friend was saying he wanted to do. I put massive amounts of attention on my clients. At the same time, I hadn't trained or equipped my team nearly well enough. I hadn't empowered them; I hadn't given them enough power to go and be strong and capable for our clients. I simply trained them to be the lowest common denominator. I trained them to standard, and that's a huge problem in the workplace: people are trained to standard.

If you've ever gone to Disney World, you know that their level of service is so far above any other business. Earlier this year my family went on a Disney cruise. My kids were four and two at the time. (If you heed any advice from this story, please don't ever take a two-year-old on a Disney cruise.) Anyway, my son, Simon, was down for a nap while my daughter, Finley, had a playdate with Elsa and Anna from the movie *Frozen*. Finley and I were walking to the playdate when she tripped on her sandal and split her lip open. We have photos of her with Elsa and Anna, and you can see she's in pain. (She clearly cared more about the photo than her own suffering—seeing her fortitude in that photo is something I'm always going to cherish.)

Immediately after the photo, I took her to guest services and told them what happened. A few moments later, a woman came out with an ice pack and a rice crispy treat dipped in chocolate (and shaped like Mickey). This was a little moment that happens all the time at Disney. Their standard is not just to take care of somebody; rather, their standard is to go above and beyond. Disney team members are trained to be exceptional.

The only way you can train someone to be exceptional is if you, yourself, are exceptional for them. The only way you can deliver unbelievable customer service is if you deliver unbelievable experiences for your team members. If we give our best to our teams, our teams will give their best to our clients. Right now, if you were to sketch your pyramid, are your team members where they need to be?

LEVEL 3: CLIENTS

We all have a dilution problem as we go up the pyramid. Things naturally get a little less potent. If I can give 100 percent of myself to my team, they're going to give 90 percent of what they have to our clients. I don't expect them to give 100 percent. It's like the game of telephone we played as kids: the original message, by the time it's gone around the circle, has changed dramatically. It's the same with service.

If we're going to give our clients exceptional service, we need to have a full tank of gas before we drive to take care of them. Does the environment you work in right now encourage you to be better for yourself, your family, your faith, and your team before your clients? If we aren't tending to the base of our pyramids, then we have little to pour into our team members. In turn, if we aren't taking care of our team members, then there's little left to pour into clients.

When work feels dreadful, it's an indication that your priorities are out of balance. In the real estate business, you can start feeling like a punching bag. Real estate is a high-risk, high-reward business. People put their entire financial future and the sanctity of their family's balance into our hands. They trust us with really big things that can cause angst, anguish, frustration, hurt, doubt, blame, confusion, and everything in between. As Realtors, it's our job to receive that exceedingly well.

I'm confident that the client isn't always right. I will always choose to stand by my team before I stand by clients. If we aren't good with our own health, if our family life is out of whack or our team tension is too high, when we need to be the punching bag that absorbs the difficulties clients are experiencing, *we're not going to meet that with our best selves.* The best way to take care of our clients is not to take care of them first; the best way to take care of our clients is to take care of ourselves, our family, and our faith first, followed by our team members. Then clients will be given the most exceptional care possible.

LEVEL 4: COMMUNITY

Bill and Melinda Gates reinvest the majority of their wealth back into this world through serving. They're caring for their communities, both locally and globally. This is the final product of a pyramid that's layered correctly. But like many of us, I have often waited until the bank was full or my schedule was cleared in order to pay attention to my community.

To be clear, we do leave community to the end because it *should* be the final priority; it should be the thing that gets the least amount of focus because the lower layers are higher priorities. But many people look at the pyramid and think, "These are all really good ideas, but it's not reality." Many of us look at the entire pyramid and feel like the first three levels take up all of our time. We think we have nothing left to give when it comes to taking care of our communities.

Yes, our businesses demand so much of our time. Yes, our clients do too. We all have excuses we use to justify not devoting ourselves to maintaining the pyramid right up to the very top. Serving outside of those main areas is often not a priority—sometimes deservedly so—because if our pyramids are done correctly we give almost everything to those nearest to us. Yet, from there, I believe that each of us has a responsibility to tend to and care for our communities.

When one of our team members left our company for another job, I saw on Facebook that she had posted a photo of her new cubicle. (As an aside, the word *cubicle* makes me shudder, but I digress.) In the photo there was a poster on the side of her cubicle that said, "You and Beyoncé both have twenty-four hours in the day."

You might be thinking, "Okay, great, but where's the time to serve our communities going to come from?" I believe that servanthood and caring for others should infiltrate into those first three levels. If we're going to care for our communities, won't we have better multiplying efforts if we do so with our families, our team members, and our clients? Then service gets into the fiber of how each layer is built.

Service is not only the thing that we do *for* our families, our teams, and our clients. It's something we do *with* our families, our teams, and our clients. Let's introduce this idea of servanthood both as servant leaders and as servants of our communities. Let's introduce it with our clients as well. Let's invite them to serve alongside us or offer to serve alongside them. Won't that create more trust and longer-lasting, deeper-rooted relationships?

INTENTIONALITY AND CONSISTENCY

You, me, and Beyoncé all have twenty-four hours in the day. The thing that's missing for most of us are those two key words I brought up at the beginning of the chapter—*intentionality* and *consistency*. If we're going to have our pyramid done correctly, we need be intentional and consistent with our highest priorities.

I started this chapter talking about how inconsistent I've been in making my health a priority. To this day, when it comes to my weight, I'm still working on consistently tending to my health as a level one priority. Heed this advice: your inability to be consistent will never get you what you want. What I want is a big life filled with abundance and love, and I want to show up in as many books as possible, whether it be a sentence, a chapter, or an entire section.

You have to be intentional about the things that show up in your pyramid—and then you have to be consistent. You can't merely show up for a smidgen of time and call it good. The practice of consistency makes you a rare breed in our society. We envy people who are professional athletes or actors because their skill is so refined. We want what they have, but rarely do we want the work that goes into it or the consistency required to maintain it.

As I write this, I've been listening to a book by a Navy SEAL named David Goggins. His ability to be focused and consistent is one of the most inspiring things I've come across. If I truly want to have a life that's worth multiplying, I need to figure out how to do so with major consistency. Running one marathon and then going back to Doritos doesn't hack it. Tending to your team by buying them nice Christmas gifts while being crummy to them the other 364 days a year doesn't hack it. Serving a couple of times a year at a soup kitchen and otherwise ignoring your community doesn't hack it. We need to be intentional and consistent with our servanthood.

To be an intentional, consistent servant leader, we must take the time to develop as leaders—while slowly and persistently building up the leadership skills of those in our care.

CHAPTER 6

TAKE TIME TO DEVELOP AS A LEADER

I grew up in a sea of estrogen, raised by my mom; my older sister, Tanya; and my aunt Anne and her four kids, three of whom are female. I was the youngest of the whole crew and was surrounded by all things female for most of my childhood. Once, the seven or eight of us went out for lunch as a family to an Italian restaurant, and Tanya received a purse as a gift. I was baffled because it wasn't a holiday. It turned out that inside the purse was a bunch of tampons. We were celebrating her first period.

That's one of my favorite stories, but it's an aside. I brought up the sea of estrogen because it contributed to my getting forced into fashion at a pretty young age, and therein lies a story that relates to leadership.

When I was a kid in the 1980s, giant bangs and Aqua Net hair spray were running rampant in my family. My cousins and my sister tried every fashion trend the mall could muster up, and there was one product called Multiples. (This is one trend I can't seem to shake—see chapter 2, "Multiply: Everything Is Contagious.") Multiples were individual neon garments that you pieced together to make your clever outfit for the day. They were advertised as "one size fits all," and they were one of the most horrendous fashion things I had ever seen.

I watched all my female cousins and my sister wear them. I learned that something could actually be advertised as one size fits all, which was and is a fashion mentality that obviously doesn't work for everyone. I'm six feet two and near three hundred pounds, so what fits you probably doesn't fit me. One size fits all is actually a farce.

HATCH REALTY TRADING CARDS

This chapter is about how we develop as leaders, and one size fits all, while common (and, I believe, misguided) in the fashion world, is also a poor leadership style. The idea of incorporating leadership as a one-size-fits-all mentality is as ironic and foolish as thinking that a one-size-fits-all clothing category like Multiples is a great fashion choice.

Instead leadership is a customized thing. We've gone so far to customize our leadership that on all of our desks we have trading cards. As a kid I collected baseball cards; now I know the stats of the people I work with. These cards have a plethora of information, starting with the person's favorite drink from a coffee shop. This is followed by their Myers–Briggs results, their DiSC profile, their five love languages ranked, and their top five strengths from the Clifton-Strengths assessment.

We've gone to such ends in order to figure out how we can empower all of our people to understand the best way to approach every individual on our team. The idea is, if I want to talk to Lindsey, one of my team members, I need to make sure that I address her by mirroring and matching how she best handles things. I need to create a customized approach with Lindsey because, for example, I know that she doesn't like confrontation. Other people want to be hit with a hammer through tough conversations; they want that kind of feedback and coaching. Some, like Lindsey, don't want that at all.

Approaching anyone with a one-size-fits-all mentality is really selling people short. I need to know what kind of team player they are, what makes them feel respected and valued, and how I can best approach them. Acquiring all of this information is a really slow process. To get customized plans for each person and have a detailed, unique approach for each individual is exhausting.

I'm confident that management is fast, and leadership is slow. We should be managing projects (standards and rules that apply to all) and leading people. Management is the quick way, but that shouldn't be how we relate to our team members. For example, you tell Rachel that she's underperforming, but if Rachel doesn't handle conflict well and you didn't take the time to really talk with her, that will lead to an erosion of trust. If you're going to go at something and you have a quick way to do it, the quick way is rarely going to be the best way.

Think of fast food. It's quick, right? But it's not the best for you. Here's another example: I remember, as a child, when we got our first microwave. To make popcorn, we no longer had to warm up the oil on the stove for ten minutes, pour in the kernels, and wait another ten minutes for it to pop, hoping we didn't burn any. That whole process took three minutes in the microwave. It was easier and it was faster, but that doesn't mean it was better.

It was easier and it was faster, but that doesn't mean it was better.

Most things cooked in the microwave aren't better. It's those things that take tender, loving care—that home-cooked meal or that five-star restaurant experience—that we relish.

SLOWING DOWN VERSUS THE NEED FOR SPEED

Most of us want to go toward this leadership journey with speed, looking for immediate results. But leadership is slow, and management is fast. If we're going to lead our people with a one-size-fits-all approach, there's a good chance that nearly nobody is going to be well taken care of. We're going to leave so many people in the dust. I can just about guarantee that if you try to one size fits all the people you have the privilege of leading, you're going to leave yourself and your team a day late and a dollar short.

Here's an example from Hatch Realty. Last year we decided to jump on the iBuyer movement. Large companies such as Zillow and Opendoor are doing this on a national level: they're putting tens of billions of dollars into circulation to buy houses directly from the consumer. They may hang on to them as rentals, or they may put them back on the market, but they're choosing to go after people who want convenience over maximizing their dollars on the market. These people are choosing to sell directly—with no repairs, no open houses, and no uncertainty. They simply know the price they're going to get, which is usually the wholesale price.

I felt empowered by a friend in the industry to start doing this with my team as well. We saw it as a massive chance for us to gain wealth, to give options to our consumers, and to grow more opportunities for our team. It seemed like a no-brainer. A year later I can look at it now and say it's working well. We're finding massive value, and it's becoming a major cornerstone of our business.

But developing it over the last twelve months has been hell. I moved so fast that I failed to allow everybody around me the opportunity to ask questions, to poke holes in the plan, and to believe that this was the best thing for them. I went at them as though a one-size-fits-all approach—what's good for Erik is good for everybody—is the path to take. I failed abundantly, and although we were able to right the ship, I had meeting after meeting to clean up the mess I had made.

I call this the proverbial "plop and drop." I think I have a great idea, so I drop it on the team, and I walk away, just leaving it there for them to clean up. Because I wanted our involvement in the iBuyer movement to happen so quickly, I ended up spending more time in triage, mitigating the damage I had caused, than empowering the next step.

> *I call this the proverbial "plop and drop."*

Instead we need to take the time to allow each person to digest what it is we're doing. Most of the world moves slower than CEOs. Most people are hesitant to change; they have questions, and ambiguity circles around every one of our "great" ideas. Too often we, as leaders and CEOs, have this idea that everything should be fast. True enough, I'm a guy who craves speed. I'm like Tom Cruise in *Top Gun*, and I have a need for speed. (Cue giant high five with Goose.) I want things, and I want them yesterday. And almost every time I've acted based on that desire for immediate results, it hasn't worked.

Leadership is slow. Management is fast. Our people, our projects, our systems need speed, no doubt, but we have to adhere to the team members who are a part of these projects. We need to mirror and match each one of those people on the team, making sure that we customize a plan that's best for them. Failure to do so is a failure to win.

THE DANGER OF SHORTCUTS

We manage systems. We lead people. We manage projects. We lead team members. To give people that kind of customized experience, it's imperative that we slow down and stop taking shortcuts.

I'll be honest: I've taken shortcuts most of my life. I've tried time and time again to get immediate results with minimal action. You name a diet out there, and I guarantee I've tried it—from Weight Watchers, to Atkins, to keto, to many, many more. Whatever crash diet was out there, I wanted to find a way to quickly lose a few pounds. I always failed, and I failed miserably, because the moment I stopped with the crash diet, I had not changed my habits.

Shortcuts have shown up everywhere in my life. Once, while in college, a buddy and I decided to order a product called the Ab Shocker after seeing an infomercial. This device was designed to be taped to our bellies. Connected to a battery pack, the Ab Shocker was supposed to turn our abs from flab into fab. Well, I had it on my belly for a couple of hours and burned out the entire device (and the majority of the hair on my belly) before the first day was up. That shortcut didn't work either.

Another shortcut failure happened just after college, and this attempt at getting quick results had more serious repercussions than wasting a few dollars on that ab device.

I had stumbled upon online gambling during college. I gambled from time to time, developing pretty keen poker skills in the process. When I went to work for the church, I took a serious pay cut—having been a bartender who made a decent living wage to a full-time worker at the church who was barely making a living. The result was that when I went to work for the church full time, I also happened to be gambling professionally.

I don't talk about this much. It's uncomfortable because I see the conflict between the two. I didn't allow the lifestyles to blur together, yet I was certainly confused about who I was supposed to be. I was making twice as much gambling as a professional poker player as I was working for the church. Gambling was alluring: it took half the time, and I made twice as much.

I did that for a couple of years before deciding to play higher and faster. I figured if it worked at the lower level, maybe it could work at the higher level too. But the game got increasingly more difficult the higher I went with the stakes. The faster I tried to play, the worse I became. I soon learned some very tough financial lessons. Speed was not the way to succeed. In fact it almost cost me everything.

I made other financial mistakes as well because I kept trying to find the fast, easy way instead of grinding and playing this life the way it's supposed to be played. A slow and steady hand is going to bring the best result. I can't emphasize this enough: leadership is slow, and management is fast. And nearly every time we try to find something that's going to give us massive returns in a short amount of time, that effort is going to result in crashing and burning.

> *A slow and steady hand is going to bring the best result.*

TAKING THE TIME TO DEVELOP LEADERSHIP SKILLS

If you think it's going to take time to develop leadership skills, you're wrong. It's going to take *a ton of time* to develop leadership skills. Not only for you but also for the people you find in your environment.

When I opened Hatch Realty in 2014, I was the guy. There were eleven of us, and the entire team reported to me. I hadn't built up any leaders. I had simply hired great people and trained them to be great at their jobs. They came from all sorts of backgrounds: we had bartenders and people from retail; we had folks from marketing backgrounds and banking. None of them (except for two people) had a lick of real estate experience. We were a motley crew, to say the least, yet we had the same foundational beliefs of how to treat one another and how to treat our clients. We all were arrive-early-and-stay-late kinds of people.

I realized that if I was ever going to scale my business, other people would have to lead alongside me. I was drowning in transactions as a Realtor, and I was drowning in leadership, too, because I was the only guy for the other ten people on the crew. When I finally admitted that it was total chaos, we formed a ragtag group of people, representing each of our departments, to take on leadership roles. (This was the first Hatch Realty Leadership Team, which I'll talk about in more detail next chapter.) They were our new leaders not because they were our top performers; rather, they were the ones I knew had a natural gift to care for those who were within their herd.

Together, we came up with a three-step training process for how to develop leaders. It's really simple, yet it's not easy. It takes time and practice.

3 STEP PROCESS FOR DEVELOPING LEADERS:

1. WATCH ME

2. WATCH YOU

3. GO AND DO

Step one is "watch me." Think about when you go to a restaurant and sit down and then, all of a sudden, you have two servers. You know immediately that the second person is training by watching the first server do their job. They shadow, simple as that. This is really basic stuff, but it's so important.

We do that whenever somebody joins our team, whether it be an admin, a partner, an ISA, or a salesperson. When I first started building up leaders on our team, they watched me make decisions. We met weekly for a couple of hours. I had a plate of decisions I was making regularly, and I would explain to them what I was doing—the angles I saw and the reasons why, giving them some business savvy, of course, but also helping them understand the mindset behind it.

I then invited them to be consultants for me. I still had the ultimate say on the decisions that were made, but I was now relying on consultants who, because they represented each department, had more proximity to the people for whom we were making decisions. We had the chance to have a better and more well-rounded decision-making process because everybody had a voice at the table.

Step two is "watch you." This is the most important step, and it's also the step that's most often skipped. The real estate world is notorious for undertrained agents. An agent may shadow someone for a little while, but what people in our industry typically do after a brief shadowing period is ask, "You got it?" And the response is, "Yep, I got it." That's where training ends.

Instead, in step two, the leader is actively watching the person who's getting developed. Again, we met as a group, but this time, after we brought up whatever issue was on the table, I would stay quiet. I was now the council they were reliant upon, but they were the ones wrestling back and forth with the choices and consequences. They would ask me for insight, but unless they were totally off course, I would allow them to come up with their own solution. I was no wiser than they were; I was simply more experienced and had been tasked for longer with having the perspective of seeing the whole as well as the sum of the parts.

This took *so* much time. A decision that used to take an hour would take a few weeks. Yet we were developing some serious leadership skills in each of those meetings.

It is in this second phase—the "watch you" phase—that the majority of the time is spent. This is fertile ground for coaching, guidance, self-discovery, and growth.

The third and final step is "go and do." That's when we send people off and say, "We trust the decisions you're making." Today, as I work with my real estate coaching clients around the country, I talk about these three steps. Once the third step is reached, no person should have more than five or six people reporting directly to them. Jesus had twelve disciples, and none of us are Jesus, so none of us should have twelve people reporting to us. We should have no more than five or six who are in our direct care.

This leadership journey is a slow one. When one of my coaching clients comes to me complaining that one of the team members they're training has failed them, it's usually the case that my coaching client didn't take the time to slow down enough to help their team member develop their own rhythm. There's simply not a fast way to develop leadership skills.

If you're going to be a marathon runner, you can't just show up and run 26.2 miles. It doesn't work that way. When I ran that marathon in my early twenties, it took me nine months of training. If I stepped away from training for a week or two, it took me that much time just to get back to where I was. Most of us hijack our leaders from consistent leadership opportunities. We have them go to the gym one day, but then they don't show up for another two weeks. Yet we expect them to be in marathon shape.

We have to continue to build upon these people and give them more opportunities to become the leaders they have the capacity to be. They can't just show up and be in that kind of shape. It's going to take a serious amount of time, and we have to be patient with that. Being a leader takes serious practice. If you want to be a fantastic leader, it's going to take a series of reps—it's going to take practice, over and over again.

And we need to create environments that allow people the opportunity to practice and get better. Think about professional athletes. An NFL player's season lasts four months. (That's sixteen games, forty-eight total hours, of football.) The vast majority of those four months, and the entire rest of the year, are spent training. Yet most of us spend one hour a week thinking about leadership and the other thirty-nine hours at our workplace in production. We're caught in the grind of our job, and we fail to slow down enough to actually develop the skills to be a great leader. This is a gaping hole in so many workplaces today.

At Hatch Realty, our leaders spend about an hour a week with me in one-on-one meetings. They also spend two hours a week in leadership meetings together. In addition to that, they have daily, ten-minute check-ins with one another. Added together, they're spending nearly four hours a week on leadership, and that's simply developing the skills for them to go and do their leadership work. Each of our assigned leaders has five or six people in their care, so they're also doing one-on-ones and team meetings. In total, I would say about 25 percent of the working week in our world is dedicated to leadership. I'm not sure that's enough, yet I do know that leadership is the most important thing we do.

THE SCHEDULED AND THE SPORADIC

If you're like me, you're looking for a couple of takeaways of how to do this. I want to challenge anybody who's looking to enhance their leadership skills to think about two key elements: the scheduled and the sporadic.

The scheduled is your regular one-on-ones, your team meetings, and your check-ins. These are really important to any organization. You follow agendas, you have tasks to accomplish, and you have to figure out if the work at hand is being adhered to. You need to help people see their blind spots and keep the wheels moving so they're continuing to grow and succeed and excel at whatever position they're in. When done right, scheduled leadership gets good results.

But I don't think that "good" is good enough. Great leadership shows up both in the scheduled and the sporadic. The most effective leaders I know are fueled with compassion and the desire to connect with people on an interpersonal level. In many ways the rhythm of showing up in the sporadic is more important than showing up in the scheduled. You have casual lunches with people or you hang out for fifteen minutes before or after a team meeting to just BS together.

Remember, leadership is slow, and management is fast. If you're going to connect only in a fast way, if you're only going to pay attention to the schedule and the agendas, if you don't take the time to actually watch the other person develop and critique them and coach them, you're going to be falling terribly short.

Sporadic connections are where relationships are truly formed. There's no agenda; there are no leadership things you're paying attention to—yet you're connecting to team members as a relational leader. As a result, you're going to better understand what's going on in their lives. You're going to learn more about what their love languages are and where their strengths lie. All of that allows you to better understand how to connect with them; it gives you the ability to mirror and match them on a better and more consistent basis. Making time for your team members, the subject of the next chapter, is both genuine and strategic.

CHAPTER 7

MAKE TIME FOR TEAM MEMBERS

When I hired the first person ever for my real estate team, I wasn't sure how I would be able to pay her ten dollars an hour. For the first time in my life, I was without a paycheck and working for nothing but commission; the self-doubt was palpable. Mariah used to be in my youth group at the church and was looking for part-time summer work. I didn't vet her, I didn't qualify her, and I didn't know the skills she brought. I simply knew her character. We started working together, and she was a great first partner. I trusted her with assignments, and she brought heart to every project.

At the end of that summer, I hired another part-time assistant. This young lady was talented and sharp, but I didn't know her at all. I hired her after a thirty-minute interview. We had a series of ups and downs, and a year later it ended not so well. Today I see what she's doing and am immensely proud of the growth she's had. We've had conversations acknowledging how messy that year we worked together really was.

Messiness often happens when you let somebody into your world without really taking the time to get to know them. Hiring someone after a thirty-minute interview is like Tinder for business. The idea of entering a long-term, committed relationship with someone after so little time getting to know them is an asinine thought. The reality is we often spend more time with our team members than with our families. It's a very painful process to bring somebody into our world and then have things shaken up in the wrong sort of way.

HIRING IS LIKE PURSUING YOUR SPOUSE

You need to treat the hiring process like a courtship. When I first met my wife, Emily, she was a college student volunteering at our church. As the youth director, I had a series of volunteers helping with the kids—a weird and beautiful conglomeration of talented people, from college students to parents to senior citizens. Emily was passionate about the kids and her faith, and I liked her immediately. We started spending time together as friends and then co-led a retreat where we took fifty or sixty ninth graders on a weekend of diving into their faith.

Emily and I worked together for six months before anything romantic happened, but in no way was it immediate love. It was clunky and complicated because we had different rhythms and had to figure out exactly what it was like to be together. It took a serious amount of time to not be just Erik and not be just Emily, but to be Erik and Emily together. We haven't lost our individuality; what we found is mutuality—where we are better together because we enhance and strengthen one another.

This is so similar to what occurs in the workplace when we partner with people. The process can't be that after one date we get into a fully committed relationship. Yet that's what the hiring process usually looks like.

Last chapter talked a lot about slowing down—how leadership is slow, and management is fast. I made so many wrong hires when I started out in real estate because I was convinced that speed was the name of the game. "Hire fast, fire fast" is a statement I heard a recent speaker make, and I loathe that statement. I don't care for "slow to hire, quick to fire" either. The idea of hiring fast is asinine, as is firing fast, because you might be losing somebody who could be great. I don't see a single benefit to hiring with immense speed. I see benefits to moving slowly and making sure that person is vetted appropriately. Bringing somebody into your world quickly is not a recipe for success. In fact it's a recipe for disaster. We deserve better, and those team members who are taking a chance on us deserve better as well.

NINE-STEP HIRING PROCESS

Most businesses place an ad, get people to apply, and then go through résumés, which can be forged, fake, or exaggerated. They look at someone's work history, rarely call a few references, and then decide whether to interview them. In the interview, they cover surface-level things for thirty or forty-five minutes and then offer the job. It's like getting married after the first date when everything is fake and plastic.

Our hiring process is different than most, and our results are also different. The vast majority of problems in the workplace will be resolved when you have the right people on your team. When you have the right squad, almost all your issues dissipate. Our issues have been plentiful at times, but the issues we have today revolve around abundance. It's a good problem to have: I have people who are too hungry and too passionate, and sometimes we have to rein them in. These are our biggest problems because we have been so intentional about hiring the right people and then creating an inclusive culture. We don't have to pull things out of people. Instead they show up ready to go every day, looking to contribute.

We came up with a nine-step hiring process that has been instrumental in making sure there is true compatibility between the applicant and our company.

9 STEP HIRING PROCESS

#1 CAST A WIDE NET

THIRD-PARTY RECRUITING TOOL LOCAL COLLEGE CAMPUSES
INTERNET SOCIAL MEDIA PERSONAL RELATIONSHIPS

#2 RESEARCH CANDIDATES

 APPLICATION QUESTIONNAIRE   PERSONALITY PROFILE   RESUME

#3 CAREER NIGHT   **#4 ESSAY QUESTIONS**   **#5 PHONE INTERVIEW**

#6 REFERENCE CHECKS   **#7 3-HOUR INTERVIEW**   **#8 VALIDATION BY DEPARTMENT**

#9 OFFER THE JOB

1. A carefully curated ad gets distributed widely, not just to folks in real estate.

2. As applications come in, we research the applicants. We use social media and networking to validate that this person appears to fit our culture. (There are rules against evaluating candidates based on people's protected classes,

and of course we make sure we're not violating any of these rules. We're simply making sure the person isn't a square peg in a round hole.)

3. We invite candidates in for career night—an extra step that most businesses don't do. The moment they get in our doors, we tell them about the nine steps and how this is going to be a different process than they've ever gone through to get a job. We tell them that our workplace is a different kind of workplace than they've ever experienced.

4. After career night we send out essay questions. There are seven or eight questions that give us a better understanding of what makes them tick. These aren't related to job experience; we're simply finding out how they carry themselves and the way in which they articulate the things that are most important to them.

5. We hold thirty-minute phone interviews. We ask about their passions, the things that keep them up at night or wake them up early in the morning. We're finding out about who they want to be in life, not how many words a minute they can type.

6. We check references, but we do this differently from almost any other workplace. For each of the three references provided by the candidate, we interview them for twenty minutes. Then we ask each of those references to give us a reference, and we ask twenty minutes of questions to that next level. Then we ask each of those references for a reference, and again spend twenty minutes with each. In total we do about three hours of reference checks. Why? The first level is their raving fans. If we want to find out the

truth or at least see other angles on this person's life and the way in which they show up every day, we need to get more perspectives. These additional reference checks prove to be essential in that process.

7. We invite them in for a three-hour interview. The first half is the person's life story, where we find out the high highs and low lows and ask questions they maybe haven't dusted off in years. During the second half, we ask about what fills them up at work—the joys they experience. *To be clear, it's not until step seven, part two, that we're asking about work.* We frame our questions to make sure people are natural fits for the tasks they will have to do in their position, rather than us having a box and the candidate formulating answers so they fit in that box.

8. The candidate meets with the entire department in a different environment—over coffee or lunch or drinks—and we see how we can connect with them. We're making sure that the department they will be working in likes them, trusts them, and wants to spend time with them.

9. We offer them the job.

Each step in the process is an elimination period. When I opened up the position to be my personal assistant, I had 307 applicants. We had twenty-five or so at career night, and then I interviewed just two of them (step 7). The funnel works!

*   *   *

At Hatch Realty and Hatch Coaching, we believe that we should hire on culture and train on skill. Skills certainly have a place in the workplace: if you're an accountant, you need to know how to do math; if you're a lineman on a football team, you need to know how to block. If candidates are going to make it past the first or second round, we're verifying that their skills align with the job, but we want to hire on culture, not skill. We all believe that servant leadership and playing for the person next to us is a better approach than me, me, me. We make sure that those who come into our organization have the same heartbeat and rhythm as the rest of the team.

CONTINUE TO REINVEST IN YOUR PEOPLE

We should treat our organizations like country clubs—the most exclusive place to get into and the most inclusive place once you're a member. That's how I run my teams. With a nine-step hiring process, the barrier for entry is clearly more difficult than almost anywhere else. We have extra steps, processes, and time commitments that are necessary on both ends. But once you're a part of our family, you have a team of people going to work *for* you every day to help you reach your goals.

We would be foolish to take all this time on the front end only to not continue the trend of immersing ourselves in their lives. During the hiring process, we're taking time to learn their strengths, weaknesses, fears, and hopes. If we put that on a shelf never to be revisited again, we've made empty promises. That's like taking wedding vows to love and support your partner until death do you part, but then the moment you say "I do," you simply go back to being all about *me* and not about *we.*

We simply cannot find out their life story and not do something with it. If our foundation is relationship building, if we believe that vulnerability and transparency are imperative, we can't just cease those things once somebody comes on board. We must continue to reinvest in our people—or there's going to be an expiration date on our relationships. The idea of proximity comes into play: not only are we working right alongside the people who come into our world, we know what's going on in their lives. Being proximate to someone means you are there with them for the ups and downs. It's a dangerous path to open up the floodgates and learn so much about a team member only to not empower your relationship to be built on helping them have a better life.

Chris Hogan says, "Good leaders help people get better at their jobs. Great leaders help people get better at their lives." Therein lies the crux of team member engagement: we know that their lives don't have to be dissected between work and personal; we just want them to have a more enriched life. We've created a more reciprocal relationship and a higher propensity for people to perform at their max level.

HATCH REALTY LEADERSHIP TEAMS

Last chapter, I talked about our three-step training process—(1) watch me, (2) watch you, and (3) go and do—and how we take an arduous amount of time to develop team leaders. When it comes to selecting team members to do this training, I don't choose to promote the people who have been there the longest or the top salespeople. I don't think those things show enough merit to be viewed as a leader. That's painful to hear for some people who have been at an organization for a long time and believe that earns them the right to be a leader. In our world that's not the case. We've made the mistake of promoting people into leadership roles because of sales numbers or how long they have worked with us—and it's never worked out. Being tenured or the top performer should not qualify you for leadership.

The people we have graduated up and who have become our most effective leaders are those who showed leadership without the title or responsibility. Leadership is a lifestyle, not a job title. Leadership is playing for the person next to you. Leadership is caring more about other people's success because that feels successful for you. This kind of leadership is rarely seen in the world today.

> *Being tenured or the top performer should not qualify you for leadership.*

In our world we had leaders in each of our departments who had stepped up and were, in my eyes, extraordinary. They were arrive-early-and-stay-late kinds of people; they were the kinds of folks you could call if you needed help moving. Prior to having the title of leader, they were already taking care of their departments. We didn't know what a leadership group was; we simply rallied together our five key people in each department. We pulled these folks together, and over weeks, months, and years, we worked slowly and diligently through that three-step training process to create an extraordinary group of team leaders.

TEAM LEADERS DO ONE-ON-ONES; CEO STAYS CONNECTED

For any organization, scaling is difficult. I've often heard the rule of ones, threes, and tens: organizations change when you move from one person to three people to ten. With one person, it's stable; at three people, everything changes; and at ten, everything changes again. The next change is at thirty, then one hundred, and so on. For us, when we went from one person to three, it was totally different, and I had to reevaluate how I was spending my time. When it was three of us, I was still massively in production. When we moved to ten people, I was still in production and hadn't yet built up other leaders. I had ten people reporting to me, and that was irresponsible.

Going from ten to thirty was when I finally moved out of production. There's a clear transition time in real estate for an agent building a team. That agent has to stop selling houses while elevating team members' production. You need to still pay the bills while letting other people step up—even though they're not as productive and don't make as much money for the company as you do. I worked ninety to one hundred hours per week, and thank goodness my wife was understanding of this vision we had together. But I had to start taking those hours and putting them toward elevating my team members and getting them to start producing like I was. We created the leadership team and went through the slow and arduous process of practicing leadership skills. It's now been almost five years that I've gone without selling houses directly to clients.

It used to be the Erik show with the Rockettes supporting him. Now it's the leadership team with me supporting them. While I used to do in-depth one-on-ones with every team member, as we grew I had to teach my team leaders how to do one-on-ones. When you hear "one-on-ones," you might think of annual reviews. That's not what I'm talking about. In fact I don't believe in annual reviews; I actually think they're really dangerous. People pile up lists of things that need to be worked on only to visit those things one time a year. That's a massively dangerous way to connect with people. Far too often one-on-ones are spent talking about what could be done better rather than casting a vision for the future.

When I would do "annual" one-on-ones (they were far more frequent than annually), these were times of affirmation and building up my work family. We talked about their goals and what they envisioned for the future. We devised steps to be taken for them to reach their goals so they could have what they wanted and be who they wanted to be. We rarely talked about business; instead we talked about the family they wanted, the debt that was weighing them down, the lifestyle they wanted to live, the places they wanted to travel, the succession plans they wanted to build, and the other things that gave them so much energy that had nothing to do with work.

When we reached thirty people, it was near impossible for me to do regular one-on-ones with the masses, so it became necessary to put this in the hands of our team leaders. Because we scaled and I could no longer be everything for everyone, I had to empower other leaders on our teams. A great one-on-one starts by getting personal. If the foundation of everything we do in our business is rooted in relationships, transparency, and vulnerability, that's what we start our one-on-ones with. We find out their energy and how things are going, and we really get an idea of how they're doing mentally, physically, spiritually, and emotionally. These all matter. In fact it's where we spend most of the time.

> *Because we scaled and I could no longer be everything for everyone, I had to empower other leaders on our teams.*

Next, there's usually homework that's been assigned to them or a challenge they need to work through, which we'll check in with later. Maybe it's a fierce conversation they need to have, a new workout regimen they're going to commit to, or a production goal they're striving to achieve. Once homework is covered, we jump to triage. We figure out what's not working or what doesn't feel right. We're spending this time trying to help address what hurts today.

Finally, the remainder of the time is spent envisioning how to make their goals a reality. We can't just learn one day a year what our people are passionate about and then not revisit it. Instead we're activating action plans for vision and growth. We're casting a vision for the future and letting them know that we want their success. It's not about our success as a company; it's about their success. That's how I'm going to win, and that's how my team is going to win every time—when everybody has their own individual success.

At the same time as I empowered my team leaders to take over these one-on-ones, I couldn't lose my connection with the rest of the team. So I've made the conscious decision that once a week (sometimes more) I have lunch with one of my team members. They pick the restaurant, and we get an hour of uninterrupted time together. I'm not talking to them about work, and I'm not talking to them about how they're performing. Instead I'm investing in them as a person: I'm getting updated on their family, I'm learning what's going on in their life, and I'm getting a sense of what I can do to give them some guidance or wisdom or maybe just be a listening ear. These lunches let them know that I see them, I value them, and I really want to know what's going on in their lives. And I do—it's 100 percent genuine. It's both strategic and genuine.

THE DISCIPLINE TO REROUTE

One final note on hiring. I've mentioned John Maxwell's answer to the question, "How do you motivate your people?" He says, "I don't. I just hire motivated people." But motivation is a tricky thing. It's often like the wind; it comes and goes and doesn't show up regularly. If we're not paying attention to what's going on in the lives of our people, if we're not paying attention to how they best receive the love, coaching, and support you want to give them, we're selling ourselves short. Motivation will suffer.

So, while we pay very close attention to the lives of our team members so that motivation doesn't waiver (again, showing interest in team members' lives is both strategic and genuine), what's even more important than motivation is *discipline*—someone who has clear-cut ideas about where they want to go. If I'm in Fargo, North Dakota, and I want to go to the Alamo in San Antonio, Texas, I can use my GPS and get a route that will take me there. I know the landmarks I'll pass on the way. But if I'm solely *motivated* to get there and I'm not *disciplined* about my journey, I'm going to run into roadblocks that are going to reroute my journey. And most of the time, we don't reroute. We go back to the place that's safest.

I want to hire people who have motivation, but even more so, I want to hire people who are disciplined. Discipline means that even if I get rerouted, even if I have a flat tire, even if I'm running into massive problems along my journey, I'm still going to San Antonio to find the Alamo. People with discipline are constantly rerouting based on things that come up. That kind of relentless discipline—someone having unapologetic passions around their goals—becomes infectious in the best way possible. It's not only imperative to have relationships with people and the mindset of deepening those relationships, we also need to have the same kind of mindset around discipline.

> *People with discipline are constantly rerouting based on things that come up.*

Losing is okay, and failing is encouraged, but we're still rerouting our trip to get to the Alamo. Every time we fail or have a hiccup or take a loss, we continue to reroute and go toward our destination rather than retreating to where we were before. It's that kind of contagious attitude within our organization that has made champions not only of our team but, most importantly, of our individual team members. We now have an organization that's not about real estate transactions. It's about trust and transformation.

CHAPTER 8

TRUST NOT TRANSACTION

Do you remember that time you got a phone call from an old buddy from high school or college? It happened to me a lot when I moved into the real estate world. All of a sudden, it seemed like everyone wanted to have coffee dates with me. I'm always a bit leery when somebody invites me out for coffee because anybody who knows me knows I don't drink coffee. If they really knew me, they'd invite me out for bacon or beers. Nevertheless, I'd go on these coffee dates, hoping to connect and build some new relationships.

Each time, they would jump in by asking me about my family, my job transition, and how everything was going. Then, thirty or forty-five minutes into the conversation—after I'd invested some in their life and their business—the conversation would switch to the life insurance policy they were trying to sell me or the new wealth management opportunity they had for me to invest in. At that point the whole thing just felt gross.

TRUST IS THE FOUNDATION OF ALL RELATIONSHIPS

I realized they weren't trying to build a real relationship. They were only humoring me in order to get to a place where I would be comfortable enough for them to ask for my business. Without building any trust, they were already asking for a transaction. It felt as though the relationship building was for nothing because it so quickly turned into a transaction. It soured the entire experience.

Salespeople walk a fine line. Do you go in for the close or build a relationship, hoping that person eventually gives you business? Early in my real estate career, I realized that I had succeeded in the ministry because I never had a hidden agenda with my youth group kids. To really connect with them, it couldn't be me showing up and being the shiniest object in the room trying to sell them on faith. It was clearly about relationship building, not about selling them something.

Being the person who has the best things to say doesn't build connection. A friend of mine named Greg Tehven shared with me some deep insights about this. He said, "When we talk about our successes, it creates competition. But when we talk about our failures and shortcomings, it creates compassion and community."

I've learned that community is formed through brokenness and vulnerability, not through boasting. If you don't believe me, take a look at a group like Alcoholics Anonymous. AA is united through brokenness. The foundation of how they interact with each other is vulnerability. You get up and say, "Hi, my name's Erik, and I'm an alcoholic." Everyone there has enough courage to say that they don't have it all together. That builds community.

Yet at work we abandon this entire idea. We think that when we come to work we have to be the résumés we've presented; we have to be buttoned up and perfect. That's one of the reasons our workplaces are so parched for connection—we're not allowing vulnerability and transparency to be the woven connections we have with people. The people I respect the most are those who are honest in their brokenness and give the most, not those who fake having it all together and take the most.

If I'm an alcoholic and you're an alcoholic, we have some commonalities that can create a real connection. But if we both work in accounting and crunch numbers all day, that's just the job we do, not the life we live or the things we struggle with. Trust is the foundation of all relationships—between alcoholics, accountants, and everyone in between. And to develop trust with people takes vulnerability, it takes transparency, and it takes proximity.

> *Trust is the foundation of all relationships—between alcoholics, accountants, and everyone in between.*

VULNERABILITY, TRANSPARENCY, AND PROXIMITY

Think about how many people we jump to conclusions about, never assuming their positive intent. Most of the people we judge have something massively transformational going on in their lives. We often fail to recognize that and are simply quick to judge. I've been guilty of that so many times.

If the majority of our decision making is only happening when we are zoomed out, then we fail to have enough proximity to those within our care. Yes, our bottom line matters. Yes, winning matters. Yes, our profit-and-loss statement matters. But do not forget—yes, our people matter too.

Recently I went through our payroll with my office manager, Monica. We were administering pay raises for a few people in her department who were doing exceptional work. I looked at the numbers across all departments and figured out that for me to run Hatch Realty, just counting salaries, is $600 an hour. In other words, to staff this entire organization costs $600 an hour. That's $4,800 a day spent just on staff. And we're a small real estate company in Fargo, North Dakota. Think about Fortune 500 companies—we're talking serious investment for our staffs.

Earlier in the book I mentioned our company's quarterly pattern interrupts. Four times a year, we close the office for a day and spend that time connecting. We laugh, we play, we get vulnerable and transparent. And we are certainly proximate to one another. We see the whites of each other's eyes because we know that when we connect and our true selves are understood, and when we can meet people with empathy, we actually go faster and climb higher.

These pattern interrupts cost the company nearly $20,000 annually—and that doesn't even begin to cover the amount of lost production from the agents on those days. That's just the salary expenses to "retreat" together four times a year.

Skeptics will read this and say, "That's going to cost me too much to close down the office for an entire day just to have a kumbaya-type experience." But that's shortsighted. Connecting actually allows us to build faster and climb higher. Hatch Realty's success is built on an environment that allows us to connect rather than just produce. In fact I believe the success we've had in such a short period of time is directly correlated to connection, to making trust the foundation of our relationships.

FRONT FACING TO THE CONSUMER

When I went to coffee with those guys, they tried so quickly to sell me something. They didn't take nearly enough time to connect; they were only interested in transactionalizing me. The result was my being turned off from giving them business.

From day one of stepping into the real estate business, I felt hungry going after sales, but I didn't like the idea of calling people and simply asking them for business. I came to learn that sales are a by-product of service. When I figured that out, I started asking an important question: "How can I bring value to this person?"

It's imperative that if we show up in someone's world, it's not to say, "Look at me. Look at what I'm doing." Those kinds of people, whether in real life or on social media, are some of the least attractive people I know. When I was first trying to grow my business, I was my own marketer and hype man. I kept shouting, "Look how great I am!" Once I stopped doing that and started building trust with people, my business grew.

No longer do I say, "Look how great I am." Instead I say, "Look how great you are." My intention now is to shine a light on other people. The way I do that is by spending enough time to listen to what's going on in their world. If things aren't going well, I embrace them. If it's just a typical day, I walk beside them. Either way I'm spending time to get proximate enough and give them permission to be vulnerable and transparent.

And I lead the way by first being vulnerable and transparent myself. For CEOs and managers, it's often a really scary thing to be seen as broken instead of somebody who has their crap all put together. Yet there is a crazy law of attraction when you're willing to be vulnerable. People are drawn to your brokenness and the light that shines through rather than turned off by you acting like you have it all together.

If you have the opportunity to serve someone with the end result being a sale, the worst thing you can do is treat them transactionally. Many movies have shown this kind of salesperson: *Glengarry Glen Ross*, *The Boiler Room*, and *The Wolf of Wall Street* all come to mind. We are fascinated by slick salespeople skilled at transactionalizing people. They care more about their commission than that person's life, so they fake the relationship and go in for the close.

It makes me queasy to think this is still happening in our world. Yet so often we're looking out for *me* before we're looking out for *we*. We simply can't be pushing a product on people. We need to be pushing service and delivering on that.

BURNING BRIDGES VERSUS TAKING THE TIME TO WORK WITH SOMEONE

The end result, in our real estate world, is that those we connect with will hopefully buy or sell a house in the future. That's a great win. But if I'm calling ten people in my database and pushing them to buy or sell in that year, I might get one win out of that. True, that would be a big success because that commission could do great things for my family and my life. But maybe I burned bridges with those other nine because I transactionalized them. I spent time talking about houses and selling instead of their family and their passions. Care more about the relationship than you do the transaction.

If you take the time to work with someone, to learn about their life, and to listen to what's going on and understand their hopes, desires, and wishes, you will learn how you can service them not only this year, if real estate is their need, but down the road as well. They may not be buying or selling a house this year, but maybe they'll refer you to someone they like and trust.

The foundation of all this is how we treat people. If they're going to trust us, we simply cannot transactionalize the relationship. The slow play works so much better. Of course we all want things, and we want them quickly. Some people make a coffee date and go for the close at that first meeting. My belief is you should be building the relationship and understanding that person's life—connecting, without an agenda, for months, if not years, if that person is going to trust you with their business.

Maybe I'm the oddball here, but my guess is I find myself in the majority that wants to be loved and respected and cared for. And when we're ready, we'll decide who we want to do business with.

FRONT FACING TO OUR TEAMS

People ask me all the time, "Erik, how many people work for you?" My response is always the same: "None. I don't have anybody who works for me. I go to work for my team members." It's my goal every day to try to help them have as much wealth in their lives as possible.

I think most leaders consider their team to be working for them. We need to go to work for our teams instead. But you can't start by just saying, "I'm coming to work for you." You have to first understand what's motivating them. And that comes from really quality conversations. You need to find out what their goals and passions are.

Simon Sinek talks about starting with *why*. Understanding why people show up at work every day is imperative to understanding how you're actually going to lead them. Again, this cannot be a one-size-fits-all approach. We must approach it with the idea of understanding their individual goals and passions.

If a team member says to a leader, "My goal is to make one hundred thousand dollars this year," most leaders would respond with, "Okay, how are we going to get there?" We should be asking why: "Why do you want to make one hundred thousand dollars? Why is that number important to you?" Maybe I will find out that their father made $100,000 and reaching that salary would be a validator of their success in life. Or maybe I will find out that they have student loans piled up, and they have a plan to eliminate their debt.

Great leaders should be able to remind our team members what their goals and motivations are simply by holding up a mirror and reflecting what they say is most important. Maybe I will find out they want a nice house, and that's why the $100,000 salary is important. Here, I would ask a follow-up question: "Why is that important to you?" Maybe the answer is "Well, I grew up without much, and I remember when my family bought our first house. That first house my mom bought changed the way she embraced life, and I saw what an impact it made on her." We need to keep asking questions, continuing to go deeper and deeper, to understand why those things are important.

Without talking about *why*, if that mythical number of $100,000 is met, most of us will be irresponsible with our money and our choices. The result? That income is still unsatisfying. It doesn't quench our thirst because we've been in pursuit of a number instead of a goal and a passion. If, as a leader, I'm ever going to understand what makes somebody tick, I have to spend enough time and go deep enough to really get to that level that *maybe they haven't even explored themselves.*

> *It doesn't quench our thirst because we've been in pursuit of a number instead of a goal and a passion.*

I have a friend who's a real estate giant. He's one of the top agents on the planet. I recently asked him if he was happy, and he responded quickly with "No." He has hit financial success most people only dream of, yet that hasn't brought him an ounce of joy. Until he figures out the *why* behind the "success," it'll still fall short. And if the main purpose of business is to make money, then he should feel on top of the world—and yet he doesn't. I believe his purpose isn't being lived out by having a hefty checking account.

When I have that vulnerable and transparent relationship with my team members—and, again, I have to be the first to model that—I have a much better chance of those people actually achieving their goals. They don't care about my goals or the company's goals; they're only truly passionate about what's in front of them. If I really want to be a chapter in their books, it has to be my job to help them achieve that. That's why, at Hatch Realty, we hold people accountable to *their* goals, not ours. Then they can really strive for it. And we're there, right alongside them, to remind them of how capable they are.

BUYERS GIVE YOU HALF TRUTHS

There's a saying among Realtors: "Buyers are liars." Most Realtors meet buyers with a lot of skepticism because they've been duped so many times. Or have they? My partner Robby T at Hatch Coaching has come up with a variation on that saying: "Buyers aren't liars. They're only giving you half truths."

Ask a buyer what they're looking for, and they'll say, "I'm looking for a three-bedroom, two-bathroom house in the north part of town, and I want to spend up to $250,000." No part of that statement is a lie. But what's happening is you're asking about what's important to them, and they're answering with numbers. These numbers are logical, but they rarely make people act. Logic makes people think; emotion makes people act. If we want to understand the whole truth, we have to understand the emotion behind the logic. I need to know the *why* of the three bedrooms if I'm going to help find the best property for them.

People are giving us half truths because they don't yet trust us. They don't trust us with their emotions; they're only comfortable giving us logic. But everyone deserves to be heard; everyone has a right to show up.

In an environment where we continue to crave more and are addicted to abundance, the idea of slowing down and diving deeper is a scarcity. Far too often in this world, our relationships only exist at the surface level. It's the easy thing to do. But that's like looking at somebody's Facebook feed and saying you understand what's going on in their life. It's a really shallow way to try to understand someone. We have to be giving them our best possible level of service by building that trust and rapport with them.

WHEN TEAM MEMBERS STUMBLE

There are times when team members make decisions that are detrimental to the company. They may fall below standard, or they may simply not be performing to the capacity they were called to. It's really easy to fire these people, but that's met with a number of consequences that we, as servant leaders, should avoid as much as we possibly can. I don't think our team members should be immediately let go unless they're choosing to fall out of culture. When people make mistakes or bad decisions, it's imperative that we meet them with two things: grace and truth.

From a faith standpoint, grace is an unlimited bucket that Christ bestows on us no matter how many times we fall short. In our working worlds, grace operates a little differently because "unlimited" grace is detrimental. What kind of relationship is that if I know I'm falling short and don't take any action to improve?

Grace means showing forgiveness and offering support during someone's trying times. We're going to seek to understand how the vulnerability in their life is impacting how they're showing up at work. We meet them where they are instead of shouting, "Fix it as fast as possible!"

It's important to note that forgiveness and trusting someone are totally different things. When I was thirty-two years old, I met with a former youth group kid named Graham. His estranged relationship with his father was coming to a head: Graham's dad had been diagnosed with a serious illness and had but months to live. I said, "Graham, you've got to forgive your dad. You've got to let go of that toxicity you're hanging on to. It doesn't mean you have to let him back into your life. It doesn't mean that you are trusting him. It just means that you're letting go of the anger."

He looked at me, knowing the obstacles and hardships I had had with my father, and he said, "You first."

I sat there frozen. "You son of a gun," I thought. "How dare you!"

Having not seen my father for nearly a decade and having completely written him out of my life, I went home that night and recognized that the advice I was giving Graham was the advice that I needed to hear. A couple of days later, I wrote a letter to my dad. It was simple: I said that I forgave him for not being in my life. I also asked for forgiveness because I wasn't always a stand-up son. I told him about my wife, my career, and the things I was passionate about.

A week later I got a handwritten letter back from him. He poured out his sorrow and shame in that letter and made an invitation to connect. Frankly I didn't want to connect with him. I didn't want him back in my life. I loved him, but I didn't like him. Nevertheless, I needed to find forgiveness; I needed to allow grace to show up in my life. I did, and I felt free.

About four months later, I was in Chicago for business and got a phone call that my dad had died. Just months before, with Graham's help, I had been able to forgive my father, letting go of all that stuff that was inside me. It didn't mean I trusted him, and it didn't mean I invited him back into my life. It simply meant that I wasn't going to hang on to that pain anymore.

When people in our working worlds make bad decisions or they fall short of who they could be, I subscribe to the idea of giving them grace no matter how hard it is. But grace does not mean that their trust is earned back. It just means that we let go of that pain.

But grace does not mean that their trust is earned back.

The longer someone is with our organization, the more grace they earn. If it's their first day of work and they arrive late, we're going to have a conversation. I'm going to seek first to understand what's going on in their life and why they arrived late. If they show up late the second day and it's simply because they're irresponsible, they're making a choice not to live by the standards in our world. A grace bucket gets deeper over time, but there does come a point when that grace may run out.

COACHING OUT OR COACHING UP

After meeting a struggling team member with grace, we meet them with truth. They have to live with the truth they created and bear the consequences of their actions. If we find ourselves at an intersection with that person, and we don't believe they are their best selves in our environment, there's a good chance that they're miserable and we're miserable. Instead of just firing them—because I don't think we should treat anyone as expendable (although moments do show up when somebody simply needs to be let go)—it's an opportunity to coach someone out.

At times it's been my job to help that person self-discover they weren't happy in our world. That process always took time, and they eventually left. There's a cost to doing that, of course: keeping a team member who isn't producing results in time invested, dollars spent, and maybe even projects handled inadequately.

But it also sends an important message to the rest of the team that if life is happening to you and you're struggling, I'm not going to give up on you. If I take the time to bring somebody into my world, my first choice is always to coach up. We're here to help by not abandoning them but instead coaching people up, diagnosing a plan with them, and working with them side by side.

If a team member comes to me and says, "I'm struggling," and my response is, "Well, go figure it out. And come back and tell me when it's better," it's as asinine as telling a homeless person, "Go fix your addiction, and then we'll give you housing." I think this is why the "housing first" model of treating homelessness has been so effective—because people who are struggling need support first.

We need to treat our businesses with that same kind of effort and care. We can't just tell a struggling team member to fix it and wait for a magical transformation over the next thirty days. We need to walk alongside and monitor the crescendo. Who they are today and who they are next week should have measurable progression that's closely monitored.

If they're decrescendoing, that has absolutely no place. But if they're taking incremental steps, we meet that with grace and understanding. Maybe they can get there in a month, but maybe they can't. For us to invest in them over the long term certainly has a cost associated with it. That cost is helping somebody's life be transformed. That cost is also my time and dollars from my business. But I believe I'll have a more loyal team member, and I'll have a chapter in their book or at least a couple of sentences I can hang my hat on and feel like I'm fulfilling my purpose.

CHAPTER 9

YOU CAN'T NOT HAVE CANCER AT WORK

One of my key people at Hatch Realty is Jim. He leads our ISA department and has become one of my closest friends. Recently he was out of the office at a doctor's appointment, and I wanted to connect with him to see how it went. I sent him a message asking him to stop by my office later in the day. He texted me back: "I'm not coming in today, dude." I asked if he wanted to talk and he replied, "Not yet."

Knowing how patient I am, I probably waited half an hour before calling him. He told me that they had found a large tumor on his right testicle. Now, Jim and I have a fun and jovial relationship, so we both had some quick anecdotes for the situation that was going on. But, jokes aside, Jim was freaked out. I was too. Jim had a major tumor that could be cancer. In just a few weeks, surgeons were going to remove the tumor along with his right testicle. They would investigate to see if it was indeed cancer, and if the cancer had spread, he would receive a further diagnosis from there.

When you have something going on in your life as private as cancer—and even more private that *your privates have cancer*—it's not usually talked about in a public setting. I'm not sure I would want my bits and pieces talked about in front of the whole room, let alone in my coworker's book, yet here I am. Of course, I've talked with Jim about this and got his okay to write about ol' righty, as he calls it. I've applauded Jim's strength and courage because he didn't hide the tumor on his testicle from us. And because of the kind of workplace we have, he wasn't forced to compartmentalize the diagnosis he was fighting. Work allowed him to have cancer.

And work responded to his potential cancer as well. We've had days where we've sent Jim home early or given him extra space. I recently went to lunch with him, knowing he would be having surgery in just a couple of days. I wanted to check in to see how he was doing, and he told me—honestly. Jim's openness reminds me of when my mom fought cancer years ago. She was not shy about it and didn't hide it. There were moments she stopped wearing her wig because it was too itchy and too hot. She was okay having a bald head and being seen as broken.

Two days before surgery, we threw Jim (per his request) a "Going Away Ball." It was a way for coworkers and friends to see him in his brokenness and show him love. And by the grace of God, Jim's surgery was a success, and the tumor was benign! He's bragging now because he's five ounces lighter and cancer free!

A lot of our workplaces don't allow for these things to be talked about so openly. We haven't curated an environment that embraces brokenness. We expect everyone to be polished and pristine instead of the person they really are. We need to meet people as individuals, which means connecting on a personal level.

FAILING TO CONNECT

We expect everyone to be polished and pristine instead of the person they really are.

My first paid speaking gig out of college was at the District Convention for Key Club. Key Club is a high school community service organization sponsored by Kiwanis that I was a member of as a student, and years later I was hired as a speaker. That first gig was a huge success. I crushed it. I had a captive room of 350 students who all breathed the same service air that I breathed, so we had commonality and common language. I walked out of that speech giving myself a pat on the back, saying, "Erik, your first paid speaking gig and you crushed it. You're gonna be incredible."

One of the Key Club students that heard me speak encouraged their high school administration to hire me, so I traveled five hours south to a small town in Minnesota to deliver a sixty-minute keynote to grades seven through twelve in a high school gymnasium. I made the foolish mistake of thinking I could just step in and automatically connect with them. As I did at the Key Club rally just a few weeks prior, I thought I would have the thread of connection woven through my presentation.

I was paid something like $250 to speak for an hour, and that was some of the hardest money I've earned in my life. Four minutes into my speech, I realized I was in big trouble. Actually, it was such a bad presentation, I probably should have given the money back. The audience was nothing like Key Club; it was students from all walks of life and levels of engagement. I had kids who wanted to be there and were respectful while I was presenting, and then there were the kids at the top of the bleachers who thought I was the biggest dummy alive. Those kids were more right than the ones paying attention.

I recognized later that I tried to sell those students on a facade. I went in having copied other speeches I had done, and I presented in the same way. It was a completely different audience, yet I hadn't changed my message at all. Speaking to a group of Key Club students versus an entire middle and high school population were two very different battles. I had to cast a much wider net. I didn't, so my ability to connect with that bigger audience was really insufficient.

When I spoke with those students in Minnesota, I failed to connect on a personal level. I gave my one-size-fits-all presentation and wanted them to meet me on my turf. I utterly failed to meet them on theirs.

LEARNING TO CONNECT

That one-size-fits-all mentality resulted in me struggling massively. I took this lesson back with me when I began my role as youth director at First Lutheran in Fargo.

I would have fifty or sixty middle schoolers at any given time, and the majority didn't want to be there. Most, like those kids at the top of the bleachers, were forced to be there. They were forced to attend church by their parents, and they were going to do everything in their power to disengage. That was when the real challenge came. If I was ever going to have an actual relationship with the kids, I recognized that I needed to connect with them on a personal level and make the effort to understand what was going on in their lives. I couldn't present to them or talk *at* them; I needed to talk *with* them.

It's the same with our team members. It was important to me that Jim knew he *could* have cancer at work. We have a saying at Hatch Realty and Hatch Coaching that stems from my experience with my mom so many years ago: "You can't not have cancer at work." That double negative leads to a positive. You can't not have marriage problems at work either...because these things follow us. If we're going to get the best out of people, we need to be able to tend to and treat the things that are really going on in their lives.

Think about the idea of an open-door policy that some business leaders have. I hear it all the time, and it seemingly falls short. The open-door policy that's universally accepted is to leave your door open for people to come to you. However, the best kind of open-door policy is to leave your door open for you to go out and connect regularly with your team. That leader should get out of their office to see people and meet them where they're at, rather than waiting for people to come to them. Which literally means meet people at their desks, meet them at their cancer. Do not wait for people to come to you with their problems. Servant leadership is proactive leadership. We cannot sit around and wait for things to land in our laps. Instead we need to go mining for opportunities to influence.

> *We cannot sit around and wait for things to land in our laps.*

Most of the time, for most businesses, we spend all our energy in triage. We're cleaning up the things that happened yesterday. Our businesses lack purpose and meaning because we spend so much energy in the pain rather than focusing on what can come from the gain. I'm not talking about the pain of what's going on in people's personal lives; I'm talking about the struggles and uphill battles that we face just from the working world—the things we have to do for business, the conflicts that come from production, or lack thereof, that creates a whole lot of energy. *That's* where we tend to spend our time connecting.

If we're going to be proactive with our leadership, we need to have a clear enough understanding and articulation of what our team members want, who they want to be, where they want to go. And we're right there alongside to activate a plan with them.

Most managers consider personal life a distraction, not an income-producing activity. Yet the seed of trust is planted when we care about our team members' personal lives. I can sit here with pride beaming from my face right now knowing that our environment has helped develop some of the most talented Realtors in the industry. They produce more and they serve better because it's not just about business. Their cancer is embraced, their brokenness is supported, and their dreams and hopes are activated. We love and serve our people well enough to not just sit back and hope that they're going to get closer to their goal. We're in the trenches with them—fighting, grinding, and hustling to make sure they have the chance to be their best selves in our working world.

WHAT WALL SITS REVEAL ABOUT PLAYING FOR THE PERSON NEXT TO US

One of our occasional activities during our day-long quarterly pattern interrupts, where we close down the office for a day and spend our time connecting, is a combination wall sit or plank. We ask people to choose one of these physically taxing activities; I tell them that the goal is three minutes and that I will let them know their progress every thirty seconds.

Everybody takes their positions and I say go. Every time, the room is fairly quiet right away. Thirty seconds pass, then sixty, then ninety. There's some quiet chitter-chatter and maybe a couple of jokes, but then the pain starts to set in. People get a little quieter. There's always an obnoxious grunter in the room who brings a nice smile to everyone's face.

Then people start dropping out. At about the ninety-second mark, we usually see some people who either don't have the physical strength or haven't developed the mental capacity to push through the pain. For those who are left, as we're approaching the three-minute mark, I'll count down from ten. When I hit three minutes, I say, "Congratulations, you met the goal," and then I watch to see what happens—because I didn't say we were going to stop at three minutes; I merely said that the goal was three minutes.

Usually, a couple of people keep going because they're determined to meet their own goal rather than my goal. We've seen people go five, six, seven, eight, even nine minutes with a wall sit or plank. They finish, people cheer, and we go back to our seats. But we're not done there.

I tell everybody what I observed, and I invite them to give feedback on what they observed. Almost always, they talk about themselves: "I really struggled, so I sang a song in my head" or something like that. We hear other comments like "I just wanted to beat Tyler." As we digest it, I ask them, "Is there a reason you were only concerned with your success?" Quite often, I hear crickets. Because unless you're exceptional, you're not going to, simply on your own volition, speak up to cheer on the person next to you.

See, this idea of playing for the person next to us that's been revisited time and time again throughout the book is something we think just happens naturally. It doesn't. It has to be a conscious decision. When you understand the benefits that come from it, making that conscious decision gets a lot easier.

So I invite the group to do another wall sit or plank. I tell them that my hope is that they can find a way to dig deeper and go longer. I tell them how important it is to encourage one another rather than just pay attention to how they do individually. I tell them that we're actually getting better and stronger when we do this together than when we do it by ourselves. I tell them that their words and their energy matter and that things are contagious when we show up to play for the person next to us.

From there, I start the clock again. And from moment one, people are cheering. It's a bit sarcastic at first, because after ten seconds of a wall sit or plank nobody is in pain yet. But the clock keeps ticking, and I watch people pay less attention to their own pain and instead focus on helping the person next to them get through what they're fighting. The change in energy in the room is palpable. And wouldn't you know it, every single time the group goes longer that second round. Goose-bump moments happen time and time again because you see folks who didn't believe in themselves change their stars when somebody else believes in them. Their tenacity is heightened when other people are playing for them.

Concentrating on your own stuff is important, of course. Foundationally, taking care of you matters most. (We covered this in chapter 5, "Priorities.") Yet there's something infectious to this servant leadership mindset. There's something infectious about playing for the person next to you. As far as I'm concerned, it's a game changer. You pay less attention to your own pain and, naturally, the tide rises for everyone in our world. When you have the ability to speak up and show up for people, there's a great chance that they're going to have more strength because of your encouragement.

*   *   *

For some of you reading this right now, the idea of opening up and letting people into the cancers of your world is so far from your core beliefs. It's unnerving for you, and I totally get that. You might have no desire to be transparent—and that's okay. I'm not saying that you have to open up. That's not the declaration I'm making here.

What I am saying is when you have the courage to open up about whatever cancers, literal or figurative, exist in your world, you're going to find that you are completely surrounded with more love and affirmation and support than you thought possible. And the strength you didn't have on your own will be found from the people playing for you.

You don't have to be the one to open up if that's not your preferred move. But I do believe we get strength from others. When we can allow those cancers to infiltrate our working worlds in the best sort of way, our ability to fight whatever tumor is going on, literal or figurative, has a much better chance at remission.

CHAPTER 10

CAP LEADERSHIP

Coaching, Appreciation, Progression

One of my favorite hires ever is a guy named Connor. I met him when he was an NDSU student hyperinvolved in leadership. I was working at the Lutheran Center on campus (during my first eighteen months as a full-time Realtor, I took on a second job as a campus pastor), and he would walk by every day, greet me with a jovial smile, and meander his way to class. He had this instant likability that I was drawn to.

After graduation Connor worked for his fraternity, traveling all over the country as a consultant. But we had talked early on in his first year after graduating about what it would look like for him to come to work at Hatch Realty. The idea was for him to lead the charge, along with one other person, of building out a new department in our company.

When Connor joined Hatch Realty, he started as a showing partner, which leads to being a buyer agent. The buyer agent role is more of a lifestyle than a job in which you punch a clock. It involves a lot of interruptions and distractions and conflict. These were all difficult for Connor to handle. Literally the most likable person in our world, Connor was one of the least effective when it came to being a buyer agent.

It was so peculiar to me because he was unbelievably smart and talented and capable. Nevertheless, he was miserable in that job. Being a buyer agent brought him no joy, and the amount of service he was able to deliver was hindered because he was simply in the wrong seat on the bus.

Part of me thought that I should have fired Connor and rid myself of the hiccup because the guy just wasn't crushing it in the job that we put him in. But we recognized that what was missing was not the character of Connor. Rather, we needed to figure out how to position him to win.

For Connor and the rest of our team members, we've subscribed to a three-piece leadership system that helps us navigate the relationships we have and creates a framework to help everyone succeed. We use the abbreviation CAP: coaching, appreciation, and progression.

COACHING

I tried to coach Connor. We tried to coach him every moment to help him become a better buyer agent. What ended up happening was I would get a bit of the runaround because he wasn't confident in the job, and the frustrations were mounting. I realized we were trying to coach a fish how to climb a tree. It just didn't make sense. I knew that the fish had the capacity to swim fervently upstream and do things that a monkey could never do. We simply had Connor trying to climb a tree when he was designed to swim upstream. It just didn't work because he was in the wrong seat on the bus. We were diligent with our coaching. We worked with every angle and aspect of how Connor could improve, but it didn't go anywhere. So we had to make a decision to position him elsewhere.

But most of our team members *are* in the right position, and they just need coaching to get better. Coaching is a big deal in relationships, and it's a fundamental piece of leadership. No matter what we do with coaching, you can't simply hope that somebody's going to get better. Coaching is and should be a time suck—but for the best of reasons. Coaching takes attention and intention. It's showing up and meeting that person where they're at, knowing full well what their goals are and where they're striving to get to, and then helping them develop a better rhythm.

> *No matter what we do with coaching, you can't simply hope that somebody's going to get better.*

If coaching is to ever work effectively, it's imperative that the person getting coached is accountable. They are the ones in charge of their success. It is our opportunity to curate and cultivate the best possible environment for them to succeed. It is our job to coach them to be their best selves. And at the end of it all, it's up to the person getting coached to do the heavy lifting.

Coaching and teaching are very different things. Teaching is a one-size-fits-all, everyone-can-do-this approach, and here is the best way to practice. Teaching a golf swing is about ball placement, keeping your head down, and making sure you follow through. Coaching shows up differently. Coaching is a one-on-one relationship where that person will stand with me, watching every intricacy of my swing, and make tweaks.

I love golf. I play two or three times a week in the summer months. My wife and I are fortunate to have a course a mile from our house, and we sneak there whenever we can. But I suck at golf. I love the game, and I'm no good at it. I can watch Tiger Woods on TV all day long, but merely watching somebody be great is far different than me going and doing what they do. The only way I can actually improve at golf is if I practice enough and if I get coached.

Coaching can't happen just once a quarter, once a month, or even once a week. That's not enough. Coaching is a regular occurrence—over and over and over again. It's not just watching over the person's shoulder; it's finding the blind spots, the areas they can improve. Coaching is giving feedback and homework and making sure people understand what's going right and where improvement is needed. Coaching is painful for both the coach and the one getting coached. It's constant. Coaching is evaluating the progression, which I'll talk more about below.

One final note on coaching: I don't think you have the right to coach somebody because you sit in the desk next to them, because of your job title, or because of how long you've been tenured at your place of employment. I don't think any of those give you permission to coach people. I think that a relationship where that person wants that kind of feedback is the only foundation for having the right to coach. You need to get someone's permission to coach them.

APPRECIATION

While coaching has guidelines—title or tenure does not automatically give us the right to coach—appreciation has no boundaries.

Whether you have a title or not, proximity or not, longevity or not, success or not...none of those matter. Your ability to appreciate somebody is a leadership responsibility we all have.

I appreciated Connor both privately and publicly for his desire to get better and his willingness to be coached. There's an important difference between appreciation and coaching when it comes to the public and private: we have to make sure we coach privately and appreciate both publicly and privately. Coaching in public is really dangerous because to coach someone means you find their flaws and put pressure on them. Most people, me included, don't like other people seeing all those insecurities drawn out publicly.

Appreciation, on the other hand, should happen both publicly and privately. Appreciation is our chance to fill somebody's love tank, to affirm the goodness we've seen in them. This is an opportunity to meet them with their love language.

Appreciation is our chance to fill somebody's love tank, to affirm the goodness we've seen in them.

I've mentioned the love languages before, but the concept bears further explanation because it's so important. I'm a student of *The Five Love Languages* by Gary Chapman. Emily and I received the book as a gift when we got married, but I didn't pick it up for years because I didn't think it was that important. Boy, was I wrong. I came to understand that if I wanted to connect with people and really wanted to make them feel appreciated, I needed to know what their love language was—how they best received affirmation and affection.

Physical touch is one. If you have relationships with people that are hugging relationships, that's a great way to make somebody feel loved. Of course in the workplace there are rules around physical touch, and permission needs to be granted. We need to proceed with all sorts of caution when it comes to physical touch in the workplace.

If someone's love language is *quality time*, limiting distractions and giving that person intentional focus is a great way to show them you care. But what if that person isn't a quality-time person? Your focused time potentially comes across as an unwanted distraction. We can't just appreciate person A the same as person B. Instead, if you take the time to learn their love language and understand what it is that makes them feel valued, you're going to have a much better chance at making them feel as good as you want to make them feel.

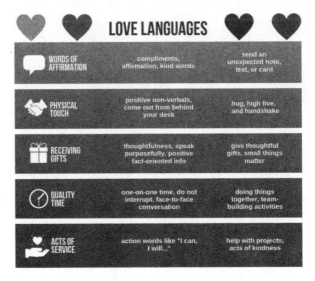

If somebody is a *words-of-affirmation* person, praising them is a great way to show them love and appreciation. If their love language is *acts of service*, you need to show up differently by serving them in some way that's meaningful for them. The remaining love language is *receiving gifts*. We need to understand the love language that our team members are most motivated by—the ones that truly speak to them and make them feel appreciated. The author of *The Five Love*

Languages has unpacked this further for the workplace in another book. It's worth checking out for sure!

PROGRESSION

The idea of progression in the workplace is often met with the wrong intention. The annual review comes to mind. In most workplaces progression is monitored through an annual review process. I mentioned earlier the destruction that I think comes from annual reviews, and I still get the heebie-jeebies when I think about them—because if I have to wait 364 days until I hear about areas that I can improve, that's unnerving for me and, I think, most people. The vast majority of us want to experience growth and feel purpose in our jobs.

I don't want to sit idly by waiting to hear about the areas where I can improve. If my take on the people I employ is right, they all have a deep desire to be unbelievable at their jobs. A lot of them are intimidated by coaching, yet they want it. They all want appreciation and affirmation, but evaluation is one of those things that is the subtle overtone in our workplaces. A once-a-year evaluation process means no one is really able to see their progression. I think that's dangerous and destructive.

I read a study recently about the ways people get satisfaction at their jobs. All different variables were measured, and the leading indicator for somebody who had a high amount of job satisfaction was the feeling of progression—that they had moved one or two or ten steps closer to their goals or achieving whatever it was they were striving for.

This could be a blind spot for many readers because maybe you don't have a direction where you're intentionally going. You're merely showing up and going through the motions. According to the study results, that doesn't create satisfaction, and I would guess that not having direction is unnerving for a lot of people who want to feel like they are progressing in their work.

If we're not evaluating team members' progression on the regular and letting them know that movement is actually happening, we are leaving them parched for purpose and growth. They might be growing, but if we're not affirming that and recognizing that, then they're going to have a lower level of satisfaction at the workplace.

Now, if they're regressing instead of progressing, we have to meet it with the same kind of intention. Any time I find myself speaking with a coaching client or one of my key leaders and they're bringing up issues about somebody at the workplace who's frustrating them or they're having conflict with, I ask the question, "Does that person know they're being destructive?" Usually it's met with silence. The person *doesn't* know because leaders are often reluctant to bring it up.

It's really easy to say to somebody, "You're doing great. I see that you've progressed. Way to go." Being a servant leader of course means that we're affirming people and celebrating them, but if that person has regressed or is not performing as their best self, we have to approach that with the same level of intentionality and respect as we do with affirmations.

Specificity matters. In order for you to captivate someone's full attention, it's imperative that you are specific about the feedback you're delivering. Generalities simply aren't heard.

My wife, Emily, is an elementary teacher. In her first-grade classroom, there are always a few kids that are more than a handful as well as many that are easier to manage. And so she and I have had in-depth conversations about how to address these kids. We both agree that she can't make overarching declarations to the class as it's common for these to fall on deaf ears. If you're needing to reprimand or redirect, the ones that need to hear it quite often tune it out. And if you're looking to praise the group, it can sometimes come across as lip service.

If I tell a group of people that I'm really proud of them, it doesn't carry much weight. Yet if I tell Kirsten how she's grown as a leader and I give specific examples—I believe that's put some wind in her sails. It's of massive importance to be specific when giving feedback.

Talking about regression and areas that person could improve is exceedingly difficult—and imperatively important. The problems that persist in our working worlds will get so much better when we talk *to* people instead of *about* people. Whether it's a conflict that's arisen or a celebration that needs to be had, we need to do a better job of studying and acknowledging this progression in the workplace. Regression is a hard conversation, yet the benefits that come from it will be high compared to the pain of sitting in discomfort and frustration from that relationship.

> *The problems that persist in our working worlds will get so much better when we talk **to** people instead of **about** people.*

* * *

Toward the end of my time at the church, I found myself sitting in an annual review in the senior pastor's office, where a giant file was placed in the center of the table. In that file was whatever good and bad I had done throughout my years at the church. It was really weird to see—overwhelmingly uncomfortable, in fact. They opened the file and talked about all these different instances where I could have gotten better, where I could have done something to increase my performance.

I was an orphaned twenty-three-year-old, fresh out of college and rife with brokenness when I started to work at the church. I was (and am) a gas pedal guy who never pumps the brakes, so I know that I mess up all the time. Yet if nobody ever tells me that I messed up or that I could be doing something better, I think everything is hunky dory. Sitting in that annual review, I had no idea of the waves and ripples and messes I had caused within the place I loved. I was hijacked of an opportunity to get better because people tiptoed around me for fear of breaking me or simply not wanting to talk about where I could improve.

I see people all the time who are desperate for purpose and meaning in their jobs. If a supervisor or leader simply helped them understand the progression they're making and where they're going, that team member's sense of purpose and value would be massively heightened. Yet we rarely take enough time to slow down and evaluate.

As I talked about above with coaching, if you do have the opportunity to evaluate someone, it first needs to be met with their permission. Getting an understanding from them that you are moving into an area of performance evaluation is an important way to shift gears. I'm usually the affirmation guy around the places I work. I'm a vision caster and an activator and a massive affirmer of people. I've learned that when I move into the evaluation arena, I need to explicitly state the different hat I'm putting on. Team members need to understand the framework of the upcoming conversation. I let them know that we're going to talk about some areas of their business that are going well and some that are showing signs of struggle. With that, we're affirming what's going well, and we're evaluating and coaching areas that they can improve.

Your team members are coming to you with this message: "Your world is going to be the place in which I can become my best self." Most are starving for our coaching, appreciation, and progression evaluations. Our ability to study the progression of our people and help them along their way will lead to them staying in our world for a longer period of time. Retention is an interesting piece in this whole business world. We talk about culture and profits and purpose. One of the key measurables, as far as I'm concerned, is retention. If we're not evaluating our people properly, if we're not coaching them regularly and helping them to get better, if we're not helping them to see the good that they're doing by affirming them consistently, then retention is going to be a massive problem.

I look at the turnover rates in real estate. The National Association of Realtors says that over 80 percent of people don't make it past two years as a Realtor. I've never not had a Realtor make it. Every one of the Realtors I've had the privilege of partnering with is still selling real estate and has had really great success. I can't help but think that coaching them regularly, showing them appreciation, and studying and investing in their progression has helped lead to that success.

Connor isn't selling real estate anymore. Instead he's now the director of training, development, and expansion for Hatch Realty. He went from underperforming to now being voted the MVP of our entire company by his peers. It took massive intention to coach him and work through all his issues. It took pouring on affirmations and love so his eyes remained looking up and not down. And we have evaluated regularly to understand his progression. He's now an asset that is earning the right to be a chapter in dozens of books. I'm insanely proud of him.

I've mentioned Zig Ziglar's wisdom: we can have everything we want in life if we help others get what they want. If we're bold enough to follow this leadership model, I'm confident that our futures are going to be filled with higher retention, much more satisfaction, an abundance of wealth, and far fewer headaches.

CHAPTER 11

SHINE LIGHT ON OTHERS

A few years ago, I posted my very first bacon meme. It was a funny quip about my adoration of that gluttonous and tasty treat. I used Facebook to send it to the masses, and it received a plethora of likes, shares, and comments. I thought it was pretty funny, so the next week I posted another. Same result: likes, shares, and comments.

As a guy who loves attention, I'm always using social media to make people smile and share with them what's going on in my life. After those two bacon meme posts, I would see people in the grocery store or somewhere else around town, and they would say to me, "Oh my gosh, every time I see bacon now, I think of you."

Somehow I became the bacon guy. I received nearly a dozen packs of bacon for Christmas one year (many from my in-laws, oddly. I guess it's better than a new scarf!). I spoke to a group, and they gifted me a membership to the bacon-of-the-month club. I emceed and sponsored the Bacon & Beer Festival for four straight years in

Fargo. This bacon thing grew to be a really large piece of my brand. It started as a joke, it made people smile, and then a lot of people in my world, when they would see bacon, would think of me.

THE 5 LOVE LANGUAGES OF BACON

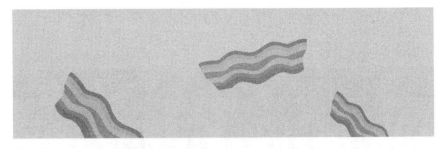

WORD OF AFFIRMATION: YOUR BACON IS DELICIOUS.
ACTS OF SERVICE: I MADE YOU BACON.
RECEIVING GIFTS: HERE'S SOME BACON.
QUALITY TIME: LET'S GO GET SOME BACON!
PHYSICAL TOUCH: LET ME HOLD YOU LIKE I HOLD BACON.

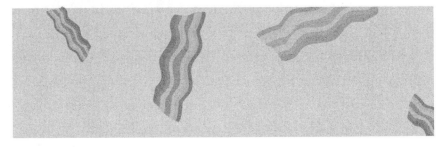

This taught me what branding was and what branding does. But bacon isn't what I want to be known for. Truthfully, I enjoy sausage as much as I enjoy bacon, but being known as "the Sausage Guy" is a little weirder. Anyway, I digress, because I don't want to be known for bacon or sausage. I want to be known as the guy who plays for the person next to him.

AFFIRMATION AS BRANDING

We are all thermostats that can easily warm up or cool down the world we're in. We know those people that brighten up a room—and we know those people that suck the energy out when they walk in. And so we have been intentional about warming up our environment by curating great opportunities for affirmations for our work family. "What are we celebrating today?" is a question we ask during every single huddle at Hatch Realty. Almost every day we dive in and ask that question. And then we get more specific and ask, "Who are we celebrating today?"

If I want to be known for servant leadership, how am I going to layer it and do it so consistently that it becomes synonymous with me? How can I be so consistent with my servant leadership that it shows up everywhere? Like we discussed last chapter—how we coach our team members, appreciate them, and monitor their progression—I have to think about if there's an opportunity to take servant leadership to the next level. If we zoom in on affirmation, then we really find ourselves in a place to brand. If we are all about affirmation and all about giving love, I believe we can use social media as a platform to cast a light on people.

When I see people, I'm known to affirm them and to embrace them not only with my actions but with my words as well. I am a words-of-affirmation guy—that's one of my love languages—and those of us who share that love language tend to give out the love that we most crave and desire. I want others to know that I see them. And I use my Facebook platform and other social media platforms to do that same thing. Once a week at least, I look around my online world and ask, "Who is worth celebrating?" I'll acknowledge

I want others to know that I see them.

someone who has gone either above and beyond or has been a Steady Betty. In these contexts I want to shine a light on these people to acknowledge the good they've done.

Here's the simple, three-step process that I pursue on social media: (1) I mention the team member, (2) I tell a story about what makes them exceptional, and (3) I post a picture. It's pretty simple, repeatable, and duplicatable. And sure enough, the accolades and affirmation and warm fuzzies I can deliver to that person are monumental. Quite often I see dozens of people from their own sphere commenting and posting, letting them know just how great they believe them to be as well. Sure enough, everything is contagious, and so we're intentional on spreading warmth.

CELEBRATE PEOPLE ON SOCIAL MEDIA

1. **Mention them**
2. **Tell a story of what makes them exceptional**
3. **Post a picture and tag them**

BEING THE CATALYST

It takes someone to be the catalyst—to actually say what others in their world are thinking. Of course, I don't believe that we should just be saying *whatever* we're thinking because half the thoughts that go through our heads tend to be negative. But there's also that good stuff that we think, those affirmations and acknowledgments that let people know we see them, appreciate them, and love them. And we shouldn't hold on to that good stuff—it's meant to be shared!

This should be done face to face all the time. It's something I try to do regularly, and yet I still feel like there's more opportunity because I don't think I'll ever grow tired or run out of giving love.

I heard long ago that we should praise in public and criticize or construct in private. Last chapter I talked about how coaching should be done privately and how it's dangerous to coach someone publicly. I made this mistake a few years ago at a real estate conference. I had the privilege of leading the group for a few days, and I was talking about how important it is for us to put ourselves and our family first and the importance of putting our phones down so we don't miss the world going on around us. And then I made the foolish mistake of calling out someone in the room who had been on their phone.

Now, this person is a friend of mine, somebody I respect with such adoration. And I made him feel so small. I didn't have his permission to coach him publicly, and it fractured our relationship for a time. Fortunately we're doing much better now because we've taken the time to reinvest back in our friendship. The idea of constructing or criticizing in public is just dangerous territory.

The idea of constructing or criticizing in public is just dangerous territory.

The flip side of that is to praise in public, to affirm and pour into those people in a group setting. I think that if I tell somebody the greatness I see in them, it's going to raise their self-esteem. They'll have a little more value, a little more abundance in their hearts, because I took the time to affirm and acknowledge them.

THE STRATEGY BEHIND AFFIRMATION

Social media has given us a pretty amazing platform to share bacon memes and pictures of our kids, but I think it can be used for much more than that. I think social media can be used to shine a light on people, to give them an overwhelming feeling of affirmation and abundance. So much on social media can be toxic, yet I'm confident that the negative can be overcome by the love we share with one another. I intentionally keep anything negative off of social media. And if I'm called to serve, and if everything is contagious, then I have a responsibility and an opportunity to share love. Yes, social media is not real life, yet if I take the time to celebrate one of my team members or somebody who's important in my life, that's a way to impact somebody else's world by me being intentional with affirmation.

There's actually a strategy behind affirmation—it's not just a whimsical idea of us being influencers and positive lights in this world. You can start doing this, too, and there's an easy strategy for you to adopt: it's called the Unsung Hero Contest, which we've done a few times at Hatch Realty. On Facebook we said we wanted to take the time to recognize some unsung heroes in our world. We wanted people to nominate who it was that they believed was an unsung hero, somebody who didn't always get the credit but was a constant value giver.

I bet that even as I'm explaining this right now somebody comes to mind in your world who's an unsung hero. We invited people to name the person who's an unsung hero and say why. We put a bit of a carrot for them to chase after, saying that we would be choosing the winner and both the nominee and the winner would receive a $250 gift certificate to the store of their choice. We had hundreds of responses.

In all our social media experimenting, the amount of love and affirmation that came to those unsung heroes was unprecedented. And here was the catch: I felt amazing, and we, as a company, looked incredible. We had a strategy to shine a light on other people, and wouldn't you know it, it reflected back on us.

BOOMERANG EFFECT

Therein lies the foundation of servant leadership—we take the time to shine the light on someone else so that when we give them strength, we intrinsically get that strength back. I want to be branded not as "the Bacon Guy" but as "the Servant," the guy who loves people, the guy who takes time to pour into others.

If I continually give, that means I continually get. We live in a boomerang-esque society, where what we throw comes back to us. You may want to throw great things out there, but until you adopt a strategy where it shows up on your calendar, you'll be falling short of actually implementing this on the regular.

For me, I've been doing this long enough that I know that, once a week at minimum, I want to shine a light on someone publicly or on social media. And you wouldn't believe the gifts I get in return. I get more dedicated and involved team members who believe in me, support me, and cheer me on. In turn I look great in their centers of influence because I'm the owner, or leader, or boss, or whatever title you want to put on it, and I'm taking the time to acknowledge that person.

I've created an energy, and since everything is contagious, I believe that person may go and do the same—thus multiplying the love that we want in this world and increasing the value we're able to surround ourselves with.

There's a poem by Marianne Williamson that has completely rocked my thinking. I first heard it in the movie *Coach Carter*, but I think it shows up in my life every day:

Our deepest fear is not that we are inadequate.
Our deepest fear is that we are powerful beyond measure.
It is our light, not our darkness
That most frightens us.

We ask ourselves
Who am I to be brilliant, gorgeous, talented, fabulous?
Actually, who are you not to be?
You are a child of God.

Your playing small
Does not serve the world.
There's nothing enlightened about shrinking
So that other people won't feel insecure around you.

We are all meant to shine,
As children do.
We were born to make manifest
The glory of God that is within us.

It's not just in some of us;
It's in everyone.

And as we let our own light shine,
We unconsciously give other people permission to do the same.
As we're liberated from our own fear,
Our presence automatically liberates others.

If you are drawn to being a light, you can choose that path by taking the time and going out of your way to be a person of affirmation and love. It means you're taking the energy to see people rather than having them see you. I believe that the light that will shine back on you is going to be brighter than the light you can hold on to.

It means you're taking the energy to see people rather than having them see you.

Back in late 2007, my wife, Emily, and I went to Las Vegas with a group of friends to celebrate the New Year. Vegas for New Year's is obviously crazy, but that's not what I remember. On the trip home, we found ourselves waiting for a couple of hours at the Vegas airport. I of course decided to grab a quick meal before we got on the plane.

My restaurant of choice was the ever-popular Burger King. I waited in line for what felt like twenty or twenty-five minutes before I even got the chance to place my order. And then I waited. And I waited. And I waited. It must have taken another thirty minutes for my food to come out—in total, almost an hour wait at Burger King. I don't remember the sandwich, but I do remember the guy who was waiting in front of me. He was unbelievably frustrated with the experience, as was I, but how we handled it was very different.

I watched this guy unload a barrage of insults unlike anything I had ever heard on a young female worker. The names he called her and the aggression he threw at her made me cringe and curl up in frustration and pain. I'd like to tell you I have a hero story of me stepping in and doing something. I don't. I watched this guy unload, and I didn't step in because I was afraid of getting dirty.

My unwillingness to step in and stand up for somebody who didn't have a voice resulted in this guy belittling and condemning a young woman who frankly didn't deserve it. I hear the phrase "innocent bystander" from time to time, but there was nothing innocent about where I was at that moment. Sure, I was a bystander, but I was not innocent. In fact I was guilty. I saw that there was something I could have done and should have done, and I didn't. To this day, I still have guilt about that moment.

*   *   *

If you're reading this now, you've made it through the entire book, and my biggest fear is that your action will be inaction. My biggest fear is that you will choose a path of doing the same thing you've been doing instead of finding at least one or two little things to implement to try to play for the person next to you. If I could go back to that moment in the Las Vegas airport, I would step in. I'm sure I wasn't the only person who felt that kind of angst and frustration in that moment. Our inaction breeds regrets far more than our action does.

Our inaction breeds regrets far more than our action does.

People are looking for leaders to step up—leaders with courage, leaders who are unafraid to get dirty, leaders who are unafraid of messing up their own lives because they're standing up for and helping out somebody else.

So many of us have a fear of getting dirty. We're not interested in other people's stuff; we have a tendency to put our heads down and stick to ourselves. Yet I'm confident that this world will be changed and deeply impacted when the brave and the bold arise. Right now, in your personal life as well as your professional life, we are parched for people brave enough to step up. We're desperate for difference makers. We're desperate for servants to come in and lead the way.

You don't have to be the strongest. You just need to know that your presence and your words and your actions have real value to them. And herein lies an opportunity: you have a chance to multiply. You can multiply love, or you can multiply hate. In that moment in Las Vegas, inaction was a multiplier of hate. There's no neutral in this world. You're either creating good or enabling bad.

There's no neutral in this world. You're either creating good or enabling bad.

If you desire to be a multiplier, the action of inaction will not suffice. Simply waiting for someone else to step up is not going to bring the change you deeply desire within you. If you're only doing things for yourself, your life has limited purpose. Sure, you may have a really incredible autobiography that other people may get inspired by. But if you choose instead to be a chapter in everyone else's book, I'm convinced that the light will be shining so brightly on other people that you'll get a sunburn…because that light is going to bounce right back at you.

If you are desiring this kind of change, if you want to be a multiplier for good, then you probably want it now. We hear the word *multiply* and think that multiplying happens quickly. I want to remind you that this may take some serious time. Multiplying is not changing everything in one fell swoop. Rather, it's slowly and methodically earning the right to pour into the people in your world.

To be a servant means showing up every day, consistently. It's not saying, "Look at me, look at me," but rather "I see you."

If you're going to be the best *you* possible, then you need to embrace being the same person in your personal life as you are in your professional life. That means allowing people to see your brokenness and your struggles. Because if everything is contagious, then maybe you need to be the first one to step up and take that chance to be open. For many of us, that may be the scariest thing of all the challenges I've thrown your way. And yet I'm convinced it's the most important one I've talked about in this book.

The other day, a friend of mine posted this on Facebook: "Somebody asked me what I'm going to do when I make it to the top. I told them I'll reach down for the rest." I'm not sure if you're at the top or somewhere in the middle. No matter where you find yourself, having your hand stretched out is the best way to both pull yourself up and help that next person along.

Right now, open your arms up. Literally. Stretch them as far as you can. Stretch from the left side of your body to the right side with every bit and every might. Did you do it? Now do it again and stretch a little more. I've done this exercise dozens of times in front of groups, and each time we find out that we always have a little more to give, a little more to stretch. It's the crazy ones of the world who climb up on a table or stand on their chair or have somebody pull their arms so they can stretch just a little bit more. There's always a little more to give.

We run at fast paces, and we're surrounded by so many opportunities and things that can bog us down. The only way I believe we can grow and inspire other people is by being bold and audacious enough to start stretching our arms out—both to ask for help and to give a hand to the person behind us.

*　　*　　*

I'll leave you with the following story.

As a youth director, I once took my kids to a church in Madison, Wisconsin. We were traveling doing mission work, and we had a chance to worship there as well as serve the congregation. They had a soup kitchen and food pantry, and we painted the entirety of it in just one day.

I remember speaking to the pastor. He showed a lot of gratitude for us being there, and we ended up talking about the idea of crossing your arms. Most of us cross our arms by putting our right hand under our left armpit and left hand under our right armpit. But as a man of faith, I know how Christ crossed his arms. And that was wide open. Left hand out, right hand out, stretched as far as he could.

That's the love and servant leadership I'm talking about. One hand should be reaching out to help someone else and the other hand should be reaching out to let someone help you. The idea is to give of yourself so freely that it inspires enough people to change the world.

OUR SERVICES

Hatch Coaching is committed to redefining how people treat people. Whether it be how leaders treat their team members or how our businesses treat our clients, Hatch Coaching is committed to providing resources and paths for all of us to be better. Learn more at HatchCoaching.com.

Follow Erik on social media to see his passion pour out—his humor shine—and some cute pics of his kids.

- **Instagram**: @TheErikHatch

- **Facebook**: Facebook.com/ErikHatch

- **Twitter**: @ErikHatch1

- **Snapchat**: @ErikHatch1

Check out Erik's radio show (Real Estate Radio) every Sunday morning on The Mighty 790, KFGO.

Have a listen to Erik's podcast called "Play for the Person Next to You."

To see all of this in action, check out HatchRealty.com.

If you're interested in hiring Erik as a speaker or presenter, please visit HatchingLeaders.com.